SIMPLY

FOLLOW JESUS

Living A Red–Letter Reality:

BECOME A TRUE FOLLOWER OF JESUS

BY TRAVIS ESCALANTE

SIMPLY FOLLOW JESUS

Living A Red-Letter Reality:
BECOME A TRUE FOLLOWER OF JESUS

BY TRAVIS ESCALANTE

SIMPLY
FOLLOW JESUS

Living A Red–Letter Reality:
BECOME A TRUE FOLLOWER OF JESUS

BY TRAVIS ESCALANTE

"LIVE A RED-LETTER REALITY"

Become a true follower of Jesus

Hello, I am Travis Escalante, and I would like to share this book with you in the hopes that you can start living out a "Red Letter Reality." My journey began at birth when I faced adversity right out of the gate. I was born with a cleft lip, which necessitated being fed with a paper cup until I could undergo the necessary repair around 6 months old. This condition caused me significant pain throughout my growing-up years as I was focused on my appearance and how people perceived me. Despite the remarkable job done to fix it, the issue lingered in my thoughts whenever I looked at myself in the mirror. It wasn't easy.

I was also born to a father who was struggling in his life as a sensitive soul, resorting to drugs to escape his emotions. Then, at the age of 5, a major tragedy struck. My mother, pursuing her dream of becoming a teacher, had a harrowing experience. One evening, after getting off the bus about a mile from campus, she decided to hitchhike the rest of the way. Fate took a dark turn when she was picked up by the Golden State Killer, who brutally assaulted and beat her before running over her head with his car, leaving her for dead in a field.

After he left, she recounted being lifted by two angels and carried to the nearest house, only an eighth of a mile away. When the residents came out, no one was there except my mother. She was then rushed to the hospital, where attempts were made to save her. Despite dying on the operating table, she miraculously found herself in the presence of God. In that divine encounter, she told God she had to come back because there was no one to care for her children. Miraculously, she came back to life, and this profound experience marked the beginning of God significantly stirring my heart.

From that point forward, numerous experiences have led me to a deeper understanding of the Spirit of Truth, who God is. The more I focus on the truth of Jesus and God, rather than the mistruths and misunderstandings of religion, the more profound and intimate our relationship becomes. In conjunction with nature and life itself, seeking God and the truth of Jesus is as simple as opening the Bible and your heart, mind, and soul to God. Reading the words of Jesus reveals a guide for living out a "Red Letter Reality." So, I invite you to "Come Follow Jesus Now" and be reunited, reconciled, and reconnected to the very essence your heart and soul perpetually long for—an intimate relationship with your creator, GOD.

May this book assist you in opening your heart, mind, and soul to the truth of God and the seemingly simple yet profound truth of living out a Red Letter Reality in your own life. May the Holy Spirit be your guide on this remarkable journey.

What people are saying about this book?

Escalante's words resonate deeply with me, and I believe they will with you as well. He reminds us it's not about complicated religious doctrines, self-righteousness, or unwarranted fear. It's about embracing the simplicity of Jesus's message: "Come, follow me."

In the midst of the chaos and distractions of modern life, it's so easy to lose sight of what truly matters. But Escalante's message is clear: we must keep our focus on the truth of who God is, as exemplified by Jesus. God is love, selflessness, kindness, compassion, grace, and mercy. It's a powerful reminder that we are called to love our neighbors as ourselves, just as Jesus taught.

In a world filled with noise and confusion, "Live a Red Letter Reality" serves as a guiding light, directing us back to the heart of our faith. It encourages us to let go of doubt, fear, and worry; instead, rest and rely on God with childlike trust. The image of a newborn baby relying on a loving parent beautifully captures the essence of our relationship with God.

So, I urge you to pick up this book, soak in the wisdom of Travis Escalante, and allow it to inspire you to refocus your life on the eternal truths of love, grace, and the teachings of Jesus. Your faith will be enriched, and your soul will be nourished by the profound message within "Red Letter Reality."

I can't recommend "Red Letter Reality" by Travis Escalante

enough. This book takes you on a profound journey, reminding us of the core essence of our faith. It's an encouragement to read that will touch your heart and soul.

Escalante's words resonate deeply with me, and I believe they will with you as well. He reminds us that it's not about complicated religious doctrines, self-righteousness, or unwarranted fear. It's about embracing the simplicity of Jesus's message: "Come, follow me."

In the midst of the chaos and distractions of modern life, it's so easy to lose sight of what truly matters. But Escalante's message is clear: we must keep our focus on the truth of who God is, as exemplified by Jesus. God is love, selflessness, kindness, compassion, grace, and mercy. It's a powerful reminder that we are called to love our neighbors as ourselves, just as Jesus taught.

In a world filled with noise and confusion, "Red Letter Reality" serves as a guiding light, directing us back to the heart of our faith. It encourages us to let go of doubt, fear, and worry; instead, rest and rely on God with childlike trust. The image of a newborn baby relying on a loving parent beautifully captures the essence of our relationship with God.

So, I urge you to pick up this book, soak in the wisdom of Travis Escalante, and allow it to inspire you to refocus your life on the eternal truths of love, grace, and the teachings of Jesus. Your faith will be enriched, and your soul will be nourished by the profound message within "Red Letter Revelation."

FOREWORD

This book was written with the intention of taking you on a profound journey, reminding us of the core essence of our faith. It's an encouragement to read that will touch your heart and soul.

Within these pages, we used the latest AI technology to help show you the truth of the message of Jesus through the red letters of your bible. AI has the ability to have a clearer understanding of the simple message of Jesus, as it doesn't have emotions as we do. So it just takes the truth of Jesus, the Spirit of Truth, and shows us the meaning, the path, and the way we are to live out the "Red Letter Reality."

In a world awash with complexity and confusion, the quest for truth remains a timeless endeavor. Among the myriad voices that clamor for our attention, there is one that transcends the noise, one that has echoed through centuries, leaving an indelible mark on the hearts of seekers and believers alike. It is the voice of Jesus Christ and speaks to us not in grand cathedrals or intricate doctrines but in the simplicity of His red-letter words.

Welcome to "Red-Letter Reality: Become a true follower of Jesus ." I'm Travis Escalante, and I invite you on a journey—a journey that shuns the convoluted paths of religious rituals and theological debates. Instead, we embark on a quest to rediscover the pure, unadulterated essence of Jesus' teachings, found in the red letters of the Bible.

In these pages, we will delve deep into the words of Christ—words that resonate with profound wisdom, boundless love, and timeless relevance. It's a journey that I, too, have undertaken, driven by a passionate desire to distill the essence of Jesus' message from the religious noise that often obscures it.

This book is not about religion, nor does it seek to prescribe a set of religious practices. It is about Jesus—the man, the teacher, the embodiment of love and grace. It's about peeling away the layers of tradition, dogma, and division to reveal the simple, revolutionary truth He shared.

In these chaotic days we live in, it's easy to lose sight of the path to being a follower of Jesus. We are bombarded with conflicting voices, polarizing ideologies, and distractions that threaten to pull us away from the core of His message. Yet, His words remain a beacon of light, offering clarity amid confusion.

Throughout this book, we will explore the red letters, those sacred words Jesus Himself spoke. We will uncover the profound depth and breathtaking simplicity of His teachings. We will see how His message holds the key to a meaningful and transformative life. But this is not a one-way journey. I will share with you not only the insights I have gleaned from my expedition into the red letters but also the questions that have arisen along the way. We will engage in a dialogue, a shared exploration of the most important questions humanity has ever faced.

So, whether you are a lifelong believer seeking a deeper understanding, a spiritual seeker in search of truth, or someone simply curious about the enigmatic figure of Jesus, I extend an open hand to you. Together, we will walk the path of red-letter revelation and, in doing so, discover anew the timeless truth that can light our way in these chaotic days.

TABLE OF CONTENTS

INTRODUCTION:

Unveiling the Red Letters

Exploring the significance of Jesus' words and their timeless relevance. The Significance of the "Red Letters" in Understanding Jesus' Teachings

The concept of the "red letters" in some versions of the Bible holds immense importance in gaining a deeper understanding of Jesus' teachings. These red letters represent the direct words spoken by Jesus, setting them apart from the rest of the text through a visual distinction. By focusing on these words, one can uncover essential insights into the core of Jesus' message and his mission on Earth. The practice of highlighting Jesus' words in red is a valuable tool for believers and scholars alike, facilitating a clearer comprehension of his teachings and their implications.

1. Direct Communication from Jesus: The red-letter approach highlights the direct communication of Jesus himself. By isolating his words from the surrounding narrative, readers

can engage with his teachings as if they were having a personal conversation with him. This directness bridges the temporal gap between the ancient world and contemporary readers, enabling a more immediate connection to his message.

2. Distillation of Essential Teachings: In studying the red-letter words, one can discern the core principles and values that Jesus intended to impart. These words often encapsulate his ethical guidelines, spiritual insights, and call to love, compassion, and forgiveness. This distillation of his teachings aids in cutting through potential theological complexities and cultural nuances, helping readers grasp the fundamental essence of his message.

3. Contextual Understanding: While focusing on the red letters, it's crucial to consider the context in which Jesus spoke these words. His teachings were often tailored to the specific situations, cultural norms, and religious understandings of his time. By analyzing the broader context surrounding these words, readers can better interpret their intended meanings and apply them to contemporary life.

4. Clarity and Authority: The red letters convey authority and clarity. Jesus' direct statements offer a level of certainty and authenticity that may sometimes be lacking in interpretations

made by subsequent writers. Engaging with his words can provide a solid foundation for understanding the Christian faith, drawing from the source of his teachings rather than through intermediaries.

5. A Lens for Interpretation: Focusing on the red letters doesn't discount the importance of the rest of the Bible but rather offers a lens through which the entire text can be interpreted. These direct words can provide insights into the intentions of other passages, shedding light on how various themes and narratives align with Jesus' central teachings.

6. Universal Relevance: The red-letter words often address universal themes and human experiences that transcend time and culture. Love, humility, compassion, and the pursuit of justice are themes that resonate across generations. By centering on these aspects, readers can extract lessons that apply to their lives, regardless of the historical context in which the words were spoken.

In conclusion, the concept of the "red letters" in certain versions of the Bible is a valuable tool that serves to amplify the understanding of Jesus' teachings. By highlighting his direct words, readers can engage with the essence of his message, distill his core principles, and gain a deeper appreciation for the profound wisdom he shared during his earthly ministry. This practice offers a bridge between the past and the present, allowing individuals to explore timeless truths that continue to inspire and guide people on their spiritual journeys.

CHAPTER 1:

Unveiling the Unhidden Truths

Rediscovering Jesus Beyond the Surface

God, our Source of Strength Beyond our Comprehension in Our Darkest Times

On August 16, 2018, my world felt like it was crumbling around me. It was a time of immense challenges and heartache. My wife and I had embarked on the emotionally draining journey of IVF, only to face the crushing disappointment of it not taking. To make matters worse, I had to make the difficult decision to let go of an employee, adding to the weight of responsibility on my shoulders. But the darkest blow of all was the revelation that my mother had been a victim of the Golden State killer—a revelation that came to light while we were at a family reunion near Sedona, Arizona.

That fateful night, I found myself teetering on the edge of a nervous breakdown. The weight of our personal struggles and the shocking news about my mother's past haunted me. I felt as though I had reached the end of my rope, drowning in despair.

But it was in that moment of despair that an unexpected lifeline emerged. My wife, my rock and partner in this storm, came to my side. She prayed over me with unwavering faith and love, and in that sacred moment, a calm descended upon me. With her support, I found solace and returned to sleep, my heart lighter than it had been in a long time.

When the morning sun broke through the darkness, we made a decision that would change our lives forever. We decided to visit Native American ruins, seeking solace and perhaps a sense of connection to something greater than ourselves. As we journeyed to these ancient sites, I carried my phone with me, not knowing that it would capture a moment of divine clarity.

There, in the vast expanse of the Arizona landscape, it happened. With my phone's camera pointed to the heavens, I captured a vision in the sky—as vivid and undeniable as any revelation. It was a vision that transcended the ordinary, a vision that I knew in the depths of my soul was a message from God.

To this day, that vision remains etched in my memory, a symbol of profound meaning and divine power. It serves as a reminder that even in our darkest hours when we feel most broken and lost, there is a guiding light, a source of strength beyond our comprehension. It is a testament to the fullness of God's presence, a reminder that His power is woven into every thread of our existence.

The journey through those challenging times taught me a valuable lesson: sometimes, it is through the darkest night that the brightest dawn emerges. It is in our moments of deepest despair that we may find the most profound revelations. And so, I hold onto that vision, a beacon of hope and a reminder of the enduring power of faith, love, and the resilience of the human spirit.

In the annals of religious history, the teachings of Jesus Christ have consistently held a central place. From the humble beginnings of a small Jewish sect to the world's largest religion, Christianity's foundation rests firmly on the life, teachings, and actions of Jesus. Within the Christian Bible, the words of Jesus, often rendered in red ink, have a unique significance and draw the reader's attention like a beacon in a sea of text. These "red-letter" texts, primarily found in the Gospels of Matthew, Mark, Luke, and John, are revered as the literal words of Christ and carry immense spiritual weight.

Yet, beyond their surface simplicity, these red letters are replete with profound symbolism and deeper truths waiting to be unveiled. In this chapter, we will embark on a journey to decrypt the symbolism within the red-letter texts and explore the hidden meanings that can enrich our understanding of Jesus and his teachings.

The Mystery of Red Ink

Before delving into the symbolism of red-letter texts, let us first address the question of why they are written in red ink. The tradition of using red ink to highlight the words of Jesus dates back to the late 19th century, with the first recorded use in the 1899 edition of the King James Version of the Bible. While no biblical mandate exists for this practice, it has since become a common convention in many modern Bibles.

The choice of red ink is symbolic in itself. Red is a color often associated with passion, love, and sacrifice, all of which are central themes in the life and teachings of Jesus. The red letters serve as a visual reminder of the profound impact of Christ's words and actions on humanity. They symbolize his sacrificial love, his passion for teaching, and the enduring legacy of his message.

The Bread of Life: Symbolism in Jesus' Miracles

One of the most well-known miracles attributed to Jesus is the feeding of the five thousand. This event, recounted in all four Gospels, tells of how Jesus multiplied a few loaves of bread and fish to feed a multitude of hungry people. On the surface, this story illustrates Jesus' compassion and miraculous power. However, when we look deeper, we find profound symbolism.

Bread is a universal symbol of sustenance and life. In the Christian tradition, it also carries deep spiritual significance as a symbol of the Eucharist or Holy Communion. Jesus' act of multiplying bread foreshadows his role as the "Bread of Life" (John 6:35). Just as physical bread nourishes the body, Jesus offers spiritual sustenance to nourish the soul.

The red letters, in this context, point to the transformative power of Christ's words and actions. They remind us that Jesus is not merely a provider of physical sustenance but a source of spiritual nourishment. When we partake in his teachings and embrace his message, we are fed the bread that leads to eternal life.

The Living Water: Symbolism in Jesus' Conversations

In the Gospel of John, we find an intriguing conversation between Jesus and a Samaritan woman at a well. During this encounter, Jesus speaks of "living water" that quenches spiritual thirst (John 4:10-14). On the surface, this passage emphasizes the importance of faith and the eternal life it brings. However, the red-letter text reveals a deeper layer of symbolism.

Water is a powerful symbol in many religious traditions, representing purification, renewal, and life itself. In the context of Jesus' conversation, the living water he offers represents cleansing the soul and renewing one's spiritual life. The red letters remind us that Jesus' words are like a life-giving spring, refreshing and revitalizing our inner being.

Moreover, the setting of the conversation at a well adds to the symbolism. Wells are sources of life-giving water in arid landscapes. Jesus positions himself as the ultimate source of spiritual sustenance in the parched deserts of the human soul. The red letters underscore the profound truth that only through Jesus can we find the living water that satisfies our deepest spiritual longings.

The Good Shepherd: Symbolism in Jesus' Parables

Throughout his ministry, Jesus often used parables to convey profound spiritual truths. One of his most famous parables is that of the Good Shepherd (John 10:1-18). In this parable, Jesus describes himself as the shepherd who cares for his sheep and is willing to lay down his life for them.

The red letters in this parable highlight the sacrificial love of Jesus. The image of a shepherd laying down his life for his sheep is a powerful symbol of Jesus' selflessness and willingness to give everything for the well-being of his followers. It echoes his later sacrifice on the cross, where he gave his life for the salvation of humanity.

Furthermore, the parable of the Good Shepherd carries a deeper symbolism related to the relationship between Jesus and his followers. The red letters remind us that Jesus knows his sheep intimately and calls them by name. This signifies the personal and intimate nature of the relationship between Christ and his disciples. The red letters emphasize that Jesus is not a distant deity but a caring shepherd who guides, protects, and knows his flock intimately.

The Vine and the Branches: Symbolism in Jesus' Allegories

In the Gospel of John, Jesus employs the allegory of the vine and the branches to illustrate the importance of remaining connected to him (John 15:1-17). In this allegory, Jesus likens himself to the vine, and his followers are the branches. The red letters in this passage highlight the vital importance of abiding in Christ.

The vine and branches metaphor symbolizes the unity and dependence between Jesus and his followers. Just as branches cannot bear fruit apart from the vine, believers can only bear spiritual fruit when they remain closely connected to Jesus. The red letters emphasize that a life lived in communion with Christ is one of spiritual abundance and productivity.

Moreover, the pruning of the branches mentioned in the allegory underscores the process of spiritual refinement. The red letters remind us that trials and challenges are part of the process of growth and maturity in the Christian journey. Jesus, as the vine, prunes away what is unfruitful in our lives, leading us to bear even more abundant fruit.

The Way, the Truth, and the Life: Symbolism in Jesus' Statements

In the Gospel of John, Jesus makes a profound statement: "I am the way, the truth, and the life. No one comes to the Father except through me" (John 14:6). This declaration, highlighted by red letters, encapsulates the core of Christian belief and carries deep symbolic significance.

Jesus as "the way" symbolizes the path to God and eternal life. He is the guide who leads us to our ultimate destination. The red letters emphasize that following Jesus is not merely a religious choice but a journey that leads to a relationship with the divine.

Jesus as "the truth" signifies the embodiment of divine wisdom and revelation. The red letters remind us that in Christ, we find ultimate truth and understanding. His teachings are not mere words but a revelation of God's eternal truths.

Jesus, identified as "the life," symbolizes the wellspring of spiritual vitality and existence. The red letters emphasize that through Jesus, we uncover authentic life in both the present world and the world that lies beyond. He is the bestower of abundant and eternal life.

The statement, "No one comes to the Father except through me," is a passage that some Christians often fixate on, attempting to impose their religious beliefs on others. However, the essence of this message is not about religious adherence; rather, it emphasizes the necessity of truly seeing Jesus and making him your Lord and Savior. This goes beyond mere words—it involves embodying and expressing your love through the lens of God's love for you, Jesus' example of that love, and your love for God and others.

Conclusion: Unlocking the Deeper Meanings

As we decrypt the symbolism within the red-letter texts, we uncover a wealth of spiritual truths and profound insights into the person and teachings of Jesus. These red letters are not merely words on a page but windows into the heart of Christ and his message. They remind us that Jesus is not a historical figure relegated to the past but a living presence with timeless significance.

When we read the red letters, we are invited to go beyond the surface and explore the unhidden depths of Jesus' words. We discover that each word, parable, and declaration is pregnant with meaning and relevance for our lives today. The red letters call us to embrace the transformative power of Christ's message, drink deeply from the living water, abide in the vine, and walk the way of truth and life, which is love.

In our journey to rediscover Jesus beyond the surface, we must heed the call of the red letters and allow them to illuminate our path. They are a testament to the enduring power of Christ's message and his eternal presence in our lives. As we continue to explore the hidden truths within these red letters, may we find deeper faith, greater understanding, and a more profound connection with the one who declared, "I am the Alpha and the Omega, the First and the Last, the Beginning and the End" (Revelation 22:13).

Modern Day Applications

Here are some modern-day examples of what we can consider doing in our daily walk with Jesus:

- Loving Others Unconditionally: Embodying Jesus' teachings to love one another as He loved us, followers can actively demonstrate unconditional love and compassion to those around them, breaking down barriers and fostering a sense of unity.

- Social Justice Advocacy: Inspired by Jesus' emphasis on justice and care for the marginalized, followers can engage in social justice efforts, addressing issues such as poverty, inequality, and discrimination to create a more just and compassionate society.

- Forgiveness and Reconciliation: Practicing forgiveness as Jesus taught, followers can actively seek reconciliation in personal relationships, workplaces, and communities, promoting healing and harmony.

- Humility and Servanthood: Following Jesus' example of humility and servanthood, believers can dedicate themselves to serving others selflessly, whether through volunteer work, acts of kindness, or supporting those in need.

- Peacemaking and Conflict Resolution: Applying the principles of peace and reconciliation found in the red letter words, followers can work toward resolving conflicts peacefully, promoting understanding, and fostering harmony in their communities.

- Environmental Stewardship: Recognizing the importance of caring for God's creation, followers can engage in environmentally responsible practices, advocating for sustainable living and responsible resource management.

- Empathy and Compassion in Healthcare: Healthcare professionals can integrate Jesus' teachings by approaching their work with empathy and compassion, treating patients holistically, and recognizing the dignity and worth of every individual.

- Educational Outreach and Empowerment: In the spirit of teaching and empowering others, followers can engage in educational initiatives, providing opportunities for learning and personal growth, especially for those in underserved communities.

- Radical Generosity: Embracing Jesus' call to give generously, followers can contribute to charitable causes and support those in need, sharing resources and spreading kindness in their communities.

- Promoting Mental Health Awareness: Acknowledging the importance of mental and emotional well-being, followers can work toward reducing the stigma surrounding mental health issues and providing support to those struggling, reflecting Jesus' care for the whole person.

- Family and Community Building: Prioritizing strong family values and community ties, followers can create environments that foster love, support, and connection, embodying the sense of community emphasized in Jesus' teachings.

- Media and Entertainment with Purpose: Those in the creative industry can use their talents to produce content that reflects positive values, promotes love, and inspires hope, aligning with the transformative messages found in the red letter words.

By integrating these practical applications into daily life, followers of Jesus can authentically live out His teachings, bringing about positive change in their lives and the world around them.

Food for Soulful Consideration - Altar Calls

The invitation system or altar call is a common practice in many Christian churches, particularly in evangelical and Protestant denominations. This practice is designed to invite individuals to respond to a sermon's message or make a public commitment to their faith in Jesus Christ. To understand its origins and whether it has biblical support, it's crucial to consider historical and theological perspectives.

The history of the invitation system can be traced back to the 19th century during the Second Great Awakening in the United States. Evangelists like Charles Finney popularized the use of altar calls as a way to prompt individuals to make a public declaration of faith. The idea was to provide a tangible opportunity for people to respond to the Gospel message and experience a personal conversion.

Regarding biblical support, the practice of altar calls is not explicitly mentioned in the Bible, as it's a relatively recent development in the Christian tradition. However, proponents argue that there are biblical principles that support the concept. For instance, the Bible emphasizes the importance of publicly confessing one's faith (Romans 10:9) and making a decision to follow Christ (John 1:12). In this sense, the altar call can be seen as an extension of these biblical principles, offering a structured way for people to express their faith and seek spiritual guidance.

Critics of the altar call suggest that it may oversimplify the process of salvation, potentially leading to superficial or emotionally driven decisions. They also point out that the New Testament primarily emphasizes personal faith and belief rather than public displays.

As I read my Bible, I contemplate the many times Jesus might have conducted an altar call if it were a practice to be followed. One of the most significant opportunities would have been during the Sermon on the Mount, where over 5000 men alone, not including women and children, gathered. Interestingly, there is no record of Jesus calling for an altar call; he simply delivered the message. I believe this absence of an altar call during such a momentous occasion challenges the modern practice, suggesting that it might be more for show than a genuine reflection of Jesus' approach.

Even Jesus recognized the challenge of commitment when some followers found his message difficult. When he spoke about the seriousness of embracing the message and making it an integral part of one's nature, akin to drinking his blood or eating his flesh, some decided to stop following him. It's easy to see the appeal of altar calls, as they can boost religious egos and create a sense of fulfilling God's will.

CHAPTER 2:

Beyond Dogma:
Embracing Radical Love

Love Unbound: How Compassion Transforms Lives

This is something that really resonates with me, as it seems we often believe we are inherently righteous and just in our thoughts simply because we identify as Christians. However, this doesn't align with the true message of Jesus. Instead, we are called to be humble servants to our fellow humans, ready to love even when it may seem undeserved. While the world teaches us to assert ourselves, Jesus teaches us to submit ourselves to others in love and in a truly radical way.

In the quiet corners of history, certain figures have emerged to challenge the status quo, daring to defy conventional wisdom and societal norms. Like beacons in the dark, these luminaries have illuminated alternative paths to truth, love, and liberation. Among them, one figure stands out—a name synonymous with radical love and the subversion of dogma: Jesus of Nazareth.

The teachings of Jesus have transcended time and place, sparking intense debates, wars, and numerous theological discussions. However, at the core of it all lies a profound message that continues to resonate: the message of radical love. This chapter delves into Jesus' subversive teachings, revealing how they shattered conventions and challenged the entrenched norms of his time.

The Revolutionary Message of Jesus

The life of Jesus is an enigmatic tapestry woven with stories of miracles, parables, and profound encounters. While many aspects of his life remain shrouded in mystery, one thing is certain: his message was nothing short of revolutionary.

At the core of Jesus' teachings was the concept of love. But it wasn't a superficial, feel-good love; it was a radical, transformative force that shattered the conventions of his time. He didn't just preach love for those who were easy to love; he extended it to the marginalized, the outcasts, and the despised.

Turning the Other Cheek

Perhaps one of the most iconic and subversive teachings of Jesus is the exhortation to "turn the other cheek" when someone strikes you. In a society steeped in a culture of retribution and retaliation, this teaching was nothing short of revolutionary.

During Jesus' time, the prevailing notion was "an eye for an eye," a principle that justified revenge and retribution. However, Jesus challenged this deeply ingrained belief, advocating for non-violence and forgiveness. He urged his followers to respond to hatred with love and to confront violence with peace. It was a call to break the cycle of violence and retaliation, a message that defied the very essence of the world's norms.

Love Your Enemies

Building on the concept of turning the other cheek, Jesus went a step further by commanding his followers to "love your enemies." This was a radical departure from the tribalism and hostility of his era. In a world rife with conflict, where hatred often begat more hatred, Jesus preached a message of reconciliation and unity.

Loving one's enemies was not an abstract concept for Jesus; it was a practical way to transform hearts and minds. He understood that hate only begets hate, and violence only perpetuates violence. To truly break the cycle of enmity, one must embrace the radical power of love. By loving one's enemies, Jesus believed that we could not only change ourselves but also challenge the systems of oppression and injustice that perpetuated hatred.

The Kingdom of God

Another subversive aspect of Jesus' teachings was his proclamation of the "Kingdom of God." In a society dominated by Roman rule and religious dogma, Jesus introduced a radically different vision of a divine kingdom. This kingdom was not bound by geographic borders or political power; it was a spiritual realm where love, justice, and compassion reigned supreme.

Jesus' concept of the Kingdom of God challenged the existing religious institutions and their rigid dogmas. He emphasized that it was not about following rules or rituals but transforming one's heart and living a life of radical love and service to others. It was a message that transcended religious boundaries and invited all people, regardless of their background, to participate in this divine kingdom.

The Parables of Inclusion

Jesus was a master storyteller; his parables often conveyed subversive messages that challenged prevailing norms. One of the most powerful parables in this regard is the Parable of the Good Samaritan.

In this story, Jesus tells of a man who was beaten, robbed, and left for dead on the side of the road. A priest and a Levite, who were considered religious authorities of the time, passed by the wounded man without offering help. It was a shocking indictment of the religious establishment's hypocrisy and lack of compassion.

However, a Samaritan, a member of a despised and marginalized group, came to the aid of the injured man. Jesus used this parable to challenge the prevailing prejudices and divisions of his time. He highlighted that compassion and love transcend societal boundaries and prejudices, reminding his audience that the content of one's character and actions matters most.

The Woman Caught in Adultery

This is a truly compelling example for us to consider. Jesus is essentially asserting that none of us has the right to judge anyone for anything. Instead of fixating on the struggles of others, he urges us to introspect and honestly assess ourselves. Too often, we are inclined to view people as inferior or believe that we know better rather than recognizing that we all fall short of God's glory. Our responsibility, according to Jesus, is to love with grace and mercy, truly seeing the other person as a reflection of ourselves.

Another powerful illustration of Jesus' subversive teachings is found in the story of the woman caught in adultery. According to the religious laws of the time, this woman deserved to be stoned to death, creating a moment ripe for condemnation and judgment.

However, Jesus responded with a profound act of compassion and subversion. He challenged the crowd, stating, "Let any one of you who is without sin be the first to throw a stone at her." This statement shifted the focus from judgment to self-examination, serving as a powerful reminder that no one is without flaws and that we all require forgiveness and compassion.

In this act, Jesus not only saved the woman's life but also exposed the hypocrisy of those who sought to condemn her. He demonstrated that love and mercy should always prevail over judgment and condemnation.

The Subversive Legacy of Jesus

Jesus' subversive teachings continue to resonate in today's world. His message of radical love challenges us to question our prejudices, biases, and judgments. It calls us to examine the systems of oppression and injustice that persist in our society and to work toward a more inclusive and compassionate world.

In a world often driven by power, wealth, and self-interest, Jesus' teachings remind us of the transformative power of love and compassion. They invite us to confront the conventions and norms perpetuating inequality and division and strive for a more just and loving society.

As we journey beyond dogma and embrace the radical love that Jesus exemplified, we are called to be subversive in our own right. We are called to challenge the status quo, to stand up for the marginalized and oppressed, and to embody the principles of love and compassion in our daily lives.

In the next chapter, we will explore how the concept of radical love, inspired by the teachings of Jesus, has the power to transform lives and communities in profound ways. We will delve into real-life stories of individuals who have embraced this love unbound and experienced its life-changing impact.

True Prosperity: A Journey Beyond Material Accumulation

In the previous chapter, we explored Jesus' teachings on wealth and prosperity, emphasizing the importance of inner riches and spiritual abundance. Now, we will delve further into the idea of true prosperity as a journey beyond accumulating material possessions. We'll examine how a focus on personal growth, purpose, and well-being can lead to a more fulfilling and meaningful life.

The Limitations of Material Accumulation

In a consumer-driven society, equating prosperity with accumulating material possessions is easy. We are bombarded with messages that suggest that more money, a bigger house, and the latest gadgets will bring us happiness and success. However, this pursuit of material wealth often leads to a cycle of discontent, stress, and a never-ending quest for more.

True prosperity, as Jesus taught, involves recognizing the limitations of material accumulation. While material comforts and financial security are important, they are not the sole determinants of a fulfilling life. In fact, an excessive focus on materialism can detract from our overall well-being and sense of purpose.

The Journey Within

We must turn our attention inward to embark on a journey toward true prosperity. This inner journey involves self-reflection, self-awareness, and personal growth. It's about discovering who we are, what we value, and what gives our lives meaning and purpose.

Self-awareness is a key component of this journey. It involves understanding our strengths, weaknesses, desires, and fears. When we are in touch with our inner selves, we can make choices that align with our authentic selves rather than conform to external expectations or societal pressures.

The Pursuit of Purpose

A crucial aspect of true prosperity is the pursuit of purpose. Purpose gives our lives direction and meaning. It motivates us to impact the world positively and contributes to our overall well-being. Discovering our purpose often involves aligning our talents and passions with opportunities to serve others and contribute to the greater good.

In his teachings, Jesus emphasized the importance of loving our neighbors and caring for those in need. When we engage in acts of kindness, compassion, and service, we not only fulfill a sense of purpose but also experience a deep sense of fulfillment and prosperity.

Well-Being Beyond Wealth

True prosperity also encompasses overall well-being, which extends beyond financial wealth. Well-being includes physical health, mental and emotional balance, and healthy relationships. It involves taking care of our bodies, nurturing our mental and emotional health, and fostering positive connections with others.

In the Sermon on the Mount, Jesus spoke about the importance of inner peace and emotional well-being: "Blessed are the peacemakers, for they will be called children of God" (Matthew 5:9, NIV). This beatitude highlights the value of inner peace and harmony as essential components of true prosperity.

The Power of Gratitude

Gratitude is a powerful practice that can enhance our sense of prosperity. When we cultivate gratitude, we focus on the abundance in our lives rather than what we lack. Gratitude helps us recognize the blessings of relationships, health, opportunities, and the simple joys of life.

Jesus often expressed gratitude in his teachings and actions. He gave thanks before performing miracles and encouraged his followers to appreciate the gifts of life. Gratitude not only enhances our well-being but also deepens our sense of prosperity by shifting our perspective from scarcity to abundance.

The Role of Contentment

Contentment is another vital element of true prosperity. It involves finding satisfaction and peace in the present moment rather than constantly striving for more. While ambition and growth are important, they should be balanced with contentment in the here and now.

The Apostle Paul wrote, "I have learned to be content whatever the circumstances" (Philippians 4:11, NIV). This attitude of contentment allows us to experience prosperity even in challenging times as we focus on the richness of our inner lives and the presence of God in every moment.

Conclusion: Redefining Prosperity and Success

Redefining prosperity and success in light of Jesus' teachings involves a shift in perspective. It requires recognizing that true prosperity is not solely measured by material wealth but by the wealth of the heart, the pursuit of purpose, and overall well-being.

It involves an inner journey of self-discovery, self-awareness, and personal growth.

As we embrace this new definition of prosperity, we can find fulfillment and meaning in the choices we make, the relationships we nurture, and the positive impact we have on the world. We can experience true prosperity by aligning our lives with the values of love, compassion, and service, as exemplified by Jesus Christ.

In the chapters that follow, we will explore practical steps and principles for redefining prosperity and success in our daily lives. We will examine how to cultivate inner riches, pursue purpose, and prioritize well-being in a world that often emphasizes external measures of success. Through this journey, we can discover a deeper and more lasting form of prosperity that brings joy, fulfillment, and a sense of purpose to our lives.

Modern Day Applications

Embracing a life rooted in the teachings of Jesus goes beyond mere dogma; it's about embodying radical, unbound reverence and love. Here are some daily practices for followers of Jesus to cultivate a transformative and compassionate existence:

Morning Reflection and Gratitude:

Begin your day with reflection and gratitude. Take a moment to appreciate the gift of life and express gratitude for the opportunities and challenges that lie ahead.

Contemplative Prayer or Meditation:

Engage in a form of contemplative prayer or meditation to connect with the divine presence. This quiet time fosters a deeper understanding of self and a sense of unity with all living beings.

Scripture Study with Open-mindedness:

Approach scripture with an open mind, seeking understanding rather than rigid adherence. Explore the context and historical background of teachings to uncover deeper meanings and insights.

Acts of Kindness and Compassion:

Infuse your day with intentional acts of kindness and compassion. Look for opportunities to serve others through a simple gesture, a listening ear, or a helping hand.

Mindful Presence in Daily Activities:

Practice mindfulness in your daily activities. Whether eating, walking, or working, be fully present in the moment. This helps you appreciate the beauty of life and fosters a sense of gratitude.

Community Engagement:

Actively participate in your community, seeking to understand the needs of others. Engage in activities that promote justice, equality, and the well-being of all, reflecting the inclusive love taught by Jesus.

Self-Reflection and Growth:

Regularly examine your own actions and motivations. Embrace a spirit of continuous self-improvement, allowing room for personal growth and transformation.

Radical Listening:

Practice radical listening, seeking to understand others without judgment. This deep level of empathy fosters connection and breaks down barriers, promoting a culture of love and acceptance.

Nature Connection:

Spend time in nature, marveling at the beauty of creation. Recognize the interconnectedness of all living things and the responsibility to be stewards of the Earth.

Creative Expression:

Embrace your creative side as a reflection of the divine spark within you. Whether through art, music, writing, or other forms of expression, channel your creativity to inspire and uplift others.

Evening Reflection and Gratitude:

Conclude your day with reflection and gratitude. Take stock of the moments of love, compassion, and growth, and express thanks for the opportunities to live a life aligned with the teachings of Jesus.

By integrating these practices into daily life, followers of Jesus can go beyond dogma, embracing a radical, unbound reverence and love that has the power to transform their lives and the lives of those around them.

Food for Soulful Consideration -
New Testament assemblies are not worship services

The assertion that New Testament assemblies are not worship services is thought-provoking, and it raises important questions about the historical and biblical foundations of Christian gatherings. To address this claim, we need to examine biblical and non-biblical historical facts and consider the evolution of Christian assemblies over time.

Biblical Perspective: In the New Testament, the term "worship" describes various acts of reverence and adoration toward God, which are not limited to formal gatherings. While the New Testament provides guidance on how Christians should meet, it doesn't prescribe a specific liturgy or structure that we commonly associate with modern worship services.

Acts 2:42-47 and 1 Corinthians 14:26-33, for example, describe early Christian gatherings where believers came together to break bread, share teachings, pray, and fellowship. However, these assemblies were diverse and spontaneous, characterized by the active participation of the members rather than a scripted order of service.

It's important to note that the term "church" in the New Testament, from the Greek word "ekklesia," refers to a gathering or assembly, emphasizing the community of believers rather than a religious institution or a formal worship service. Early Christians met in homes, not grand cathedrals, suggesting an informal and communal approach to their faith.

Historical Development: The formalization of worship services as we know them today can be traced back to the early centuries of the Christian Church. As Christianity gained official recognition in the Roman Empire, Christian gatherings became more organized and structured. Liturgical elements, clerical roles, and a designated order of worship gradually evolved.

The Nicene Creed (325 AD) and the Council of Chalcedon (451 AD) were pivotal in shaping Christian theology and liturgy. The development of the Eucharist or Mass in the Western Christian tradition and the Divine Liturgy in the Eastern Christian tradition further solidified the idea of formal worship services.

This historical progression suggests that the New Testament assemblies, characterized by simplicity and active participation, gradually evolved into more structured worship services as the Church grew and adapted to its changing circumstances.

Contemporary Interpretations: Today, the form of Christian assemblies varies widely. Some churches maintain a highly liturgical, formal worship service, while others follow a more spontaneous and informal model. Many Protestant denominations emphasize the preaching of the Word and congregational singing, but they differ in style and tradition. The assertion that New Testament assemblies are not worship services may resonate with those who aim to reclaim the simplicity and communal aspects of early Christian gatherings. This perspective underscores that the essence of Christian faith lies in the relationship with God and the fellowship among believers, prioritizing these aspects over ritualistic worship practices.

In conclusion, whether New Testament assemblies are considered worship services depends on one's interpretation of biblical texts and historical context. The New Testament provides guidance on the principles of Christian gatherings but does not prescribe a rigid format. As the Christian Church evolved over time, it incorporated various liturgical elements and developed formal worship services. Modern Christian practices encompass a broad spectrum, from high liturgy to informal gatherings, reflecting the diversity of interpretations and historical developments within the faith.

As I read the Bible and encourage you to do the same, Jesus clearly instructs us to actively live out and spread the GOOD NEWS. He provides guidance on how to do this, reiterating it multiple times. Importantly, Jesus never intended for this mission to become a formulaic system. Instead, he envisioned it as a daily embodiment of God's love.

This involved meeting together in various settings—homes, fields, sides of the road, or anywhere for that matter. I don't see Jesus endorsing the idea of buildings sitting empty for most of the week when they could be utilized to house and shelter people in need. Instead, he seems to advocate for a dynamic and practical application of faith—one that extends beyond the confines of structured spaces.

CHAPTER 3:

The Parables You Never Knew

Decoding Wisdom: Finding Modern Lessons in Ancient Stories

Decoding the wisdom of Jesus can be challenging unless we keep our focus on the truth of who Jesus is. It's easy to get stuck in the routine of making it from Sunday to Sunday without truly experiencing the fullness that God intended for each of us through the life of Jesus.

To grasp the richness of the message, we must center our lives on seeking God with all our hearts, minds, and souls—an imperative emphasized by Jesus in one of the great commandments of God.

But what does this look like? Firstly, we need to break free from our knowledge of good and evil thinking, which essentially means ceasing to play God. Then, we should open our hearts, minds, and souls to the gift of Jesus' simple message, as written in the Red Letters of our Bible and demonstrated through his life. Jesus shows us the way, the truth, and the life.

So, as you continue reading, let go of your preconceived notions and ask God to help open your heart, mind, and soul to the fullness that God desires for and with you.

In this chapter of "The Parables You Never Knew," we've embarked on a journey of discovery, unveiling the profound wisdom hidden within ancient stories. We've explored how these parables can serve as timeless guides for navigating the complexities of our lives. Now, as we delve deeper into our exploration, we shift our focus from decoding wisdom to applying it.

The Relevance of Parables in the Modern World

The parables of old, often attributed to the teachings of Jesus, have an enduring quality that transcends time and place. Their power lies in their simplicity yet profound ability to convey essential truths. In this chapter, we will explore how these age-old parables can still serve as beacons of light in our increasingly complex and fast-paced modern world.

The Ethos of Kingdom Values

To understand how these parables can be applied in our contemporary lives, we must first grasp the ethos of Kingdom values. The Kingdom of God, as described in the parables, represents a realm of divine justice, compassion, and righteousness. It is a kingdom where the poor are blessed, the meek inherit the earth, and the peacemakers are called children of God.

This ethos challenges us to question the prevailing values of our society and encourages us to seek a higher standard. It calls us to be stewards of love, kindness, and justice, even in a world that often seems dominated by self-interest and materialism.

The Good Samaritan - A Call to Compassion

Luke 10:29–37

The parable of the Good Samaritan illustrates the essence of compassion and love for one's neighbor. In a world where divisions and prejudices still exist, this parable is a powerful reminder of our duty to care for those in need, regardless of their background.

Modern Application: In our modern world, marked by divisive politics and social inequalities, the Good Samaritan challenges us to break down barriers and extend a helping hand to those suffering. It reminds us that compassion knows no boundaries and that kindness should be our default response to the suffering of others.

We can apply this parable by volunteering our time at local shelters, supporting charitable organizations, or simply being more attentive to the needs of our neighbors. In doing so, we live out the Kingdom value of love for one another.

The Prodigal Son - Embracing Forgiveness and Redemption

Luke 10:29–37 Luke 15:11-32

The story of the Prodigal Son is a tale of redemption and forgiveness. In a world where grudges and resentment often fester, this parable calls us to extend forgiveness, no matter how deep the wounds may be.

Modern Application: In a society where canceled culture and social media outrage can quickly escalate, the Prodigal Son invites us to practice forgiveness and reconciliation. It encourages us to look beyond past mistakes and see the potential for transformation in every person.

We can apply this parable by mending broken relationships, practicing forgiveness in our personal lives, and advocating for restorative justice in our communities. By doing so, we embody the Kingdom value of reconciliation and offer hope for a better future.

The Mustard Seed - Cultivating Faith and Growth

Matthew 13:31–32, Mark 4:30–32, and Luke 13:18–19

The parable of the Mustard Seed teaches us that even the smallest acts of faith can yield remarkable growth. In a world filled with doubt and cynicism, this parable reminds us of the power of belief and persistence.

Modern Application: In our fast-paced, instant-gratification culture, the Mustard Seed challenges us to have patience and faith in the process. It encourages us to start small, knowing that our efforts can lead to significant change, no matter how modest.

We can apply this parable by pursuing our dreams and aspirations, even when they seem daunting. It also reminds us to support and encourage others in their endeavors, recognizing the potential for greatness in the seemingly insignificant.

The Talents - Maximizing Our Gifts for the Common Good

Matthew 25:14-30

The parable of the Talents teaches us about stewardship and the responsibility to maximize our gifts and abilities for the common good. In a world driven by individual success and competition, this parable challenges us to shift our focus toward community and collaboration.

Modern Application: In a society where success is often measured by personal achievement, the Talents parable encourages us to use our talents and resources for the betterment of society. It calls us to seek ways to uplift others and make a positive impact on our communities.

We can apply this parable by volunteering our skills to support local initiatives, mentoring others to help them reach their full potential, and advocating for policies that promote social justice and equality.

The Lost Sheep - Pursuing the Lost and Marginalized

Matthew 18:12–14 Luke 15:3–7

The parable of the Lost Sheep emphasizes the importance of seeking out and caring for marginalized or lost people. In a world where many individuals and groups are marginalized and overlooked, this parable calls us to be advocates for justice and inclusion.

Modern Application: In a world marked by discrimination, prejudice, and exclusion, the Lost Sheep parable urges us to stand up for the rights and dignity of those who are marginalized. It compels us to actively seek out those who are lost and offer them support and compassion.

We can apply this parable by engaging in activism, supporting marginalized communities, and working to eliminate systemic injustices. It reminds us that the Kingdom's values of justice and equality should guide our actions and decisions.

The Unforgiving Servant - The Importance of Mercy and Grace

Matthew 18:21-35

The parable of the Unforgiving Servant underscores the significance of showing mercy and grace to others, just as we have received it ourselves. In a world where judgment and condemnation are often prevalent, this parable challenges us to extend forgiveness and compassion.

Modern Application: In a culture where blame and judgment are rampant, the Unforgiving Servant teaches us to cultivate a spirit of forgiveness and understanding. It prompts us to recognize our own imperfections and extend grace to those who have wronged us.

We can apply this parable by practicing forgiveness in our personal lives, supporting restorative justice initiatives, and advocating for policies prioritizing rehabilitation over punishment. It reminds us that the Kingdom's values of mercy and grace should be reflected in our interactions with others.

The Pearl of Great Price - The Search for True Value

Matthew 13:45-46

The parable of the Pearl of Great Price highlights the pursuit of true value and meaning in life. In a world where materialism and consumerism often dominate, this parable encourages us to seek the treasures of the heart and soul.

Modern Application: In a society where the relentless pursuit of material wealth and status can lead to emptiness and discontent, the Pearl of Great Price challenges us to reevaluate our priorities. It prompts us to seek fulfillment and purpose in what truly matters.

We can apply this parable by embracing a minimalist lifestyle, focusing on relationships and experiences over possessions, and dedicating ourselves to meaningful causes. It reminds us that the

Kingdom's inner richness and contentment values are far more valuable than worldly wealth.

The Rich Fool - The Danger of Greed and Selfishness

Luke 12:13-21

The parable of the Rich Fool warns against the dangers of greed and selfishness. In a world where the pursuit of wealth and power often takes precedence, this parable reminds us of the importance of generosity and concern.

Modern Application: In a culture that often glorifies material success and personal gain, the Rich Fool parable calls us to be mindful of the impact of our actions on others. It prompts us to consider the needs of the less fortunate and to use our resources for the greater good.

We can apply this parable by practicing generosity, supporting charitable organizations, and advocating for economic fairness and social justice policies. It reminds us that the Kingdom values of compassion and selflessness should guide our choices and priorities.

Conclusion: Living Parables in a Modern World

The parables you never knew have a timeless relevance that transcends the boundaries of time and culture. They offer a blueprint for living out the Kingdom's values of love, compassion, justice, and grace in our contemporary world. As we apply these ancient stories to our modern lives, we become agents of positive change, bringing light to the darkness and hope to the despairing.

In the hustle and bustle of our fast-paced lives, the parables gently remind us what truly matters. They challenge us to look beyond the surface of our existence and strive for a deeper, more meaningful connection with ourselves and others. By embracing these parables and living out their wisdom, we can transform our world into a more just, compassionate, and loving place—a world that reflects the ethos of Kingdom values.

Modern Day Applications

Understanding and decoding the wisdom embedded in the parables of Jesus requires a thoughtful and reflective approach. Here are some ways to better understand and extract modern lessons from these ancient stories:

Cultural Context:

Research the historical and cultural context in which Jesus lived. Understanding the customs, traditions, and societal norms of that time can provide valuable insights into the parables.

Symbolism and Metaphors:

Recognize the symbolic nature of the parables. Many of Jesus' teachings are presented in metaphorical language. Identify the key elements and symbols within each parable and explore their deeper meanings.

Relate to Everyday Life:

Connect the parables to contemporary issues and everyday life. Consider how the principles conveyed in the parables can be applied to modern challenges, ethical dilemmas, and interpersonal relationships.

Ask Questions:

Engage with the text by asking questions. What is the central message? How do the characters and their actions relate to real-life situations? What moral or ethical lessons can be derived?

Compare and Contrast:

Compare different parables to find common themes and messages. By identifying recurring motifs, you can better understand the principles Jesus sought to convey.

Contextualize with Other Scriptures:

Cross-reference the parables with other biblical passages. This can provide a more comprehensive understanding of the broader biblical message and how the parables fit into the larger narrative.

Consider the Audience:

Reflect on the original audience of Jesus' teachings. How would they have interpreted the parables? Understanding the intended message for that audience can shed light on the timeless wisdom contained in the stories.

Prayer and Meditation:

Take time for prayer and meditation on the parables. Quiet reflection can open your mind to deeper spiritual insights and help you internalize the moral teachings.

Study Historical Commentaries:

Explore commentaries and interpretations by scholars and theologians throughout history. Understanding how various thinkers have interpreted the parables can offer diverse perspectives.

Personal Application:

Consider how the lessons from the parables can be practically applied in your own life. What changes can you make in your attitudes, behaviors, and relationships based on the wisdom found in the parables?

Community Discussion:

Engage in discussions with others, such as in a study group or church setting. Hearing different viewpoints can enhance your understanding and provide new insights into the parables.

Read Parables in Parallel Cultures:

Explore parables or stories from other cultures and religions. Drawing parallels between cultural narratives can deepen your understanding of universal truths and values.

Approaching the parables with a combination of historical awareness, symbolic interpretation, and a commitment to personal reflection can help unlock their timeless wisdom and relevance for modern life.

Food for Soulful Consideration - The New Testament teaches nothing about a clergy, and the prevalent clergy/laity distinction runs counter to Scripture alone

The statement that "The New Testament teaches nothing about a clergy, and the prevalent clergy/laity distinction runs counter to Scripture alone" is a perspective put forth by some individuals and religious groups, primarily within the context of Protestant Christianity. Let's examine this assertion in light of biblical and non-biblical historical facts.

Biblical Perspective:

Early Christian Community: In the early Christian community, as depicted in the New Testament, there is indeed no explicit mention of a formal clergy system akin to what is found in many modern denominations. The apostles and other leaders played a central role in teaching and guiding the church. But the terms "clergy" and "laity" as we understand them today are absent in the New Testament.

Servant Leadership: The New Testament emphasizes a model of leadership that focuses on servanthood, humility, and the gifting of the Holy Spirit. Jesus' teachings in the Gospels and the writings of Paul stress the importance of love, service, and the equality of all believers.

Priesthood of All Believers: Many proponents of the statement point to the idea of the "priesthood of all believers," a concept derived from passages like 1 Peter 2:9, which suggests that all Christians have direct access to God and a role in the ministry. They argue that this undermines the need for a distinct clergy class.

Historical Development:

Emergence of Clergy: The development of a distinct clergy can be traced to the post-apostolic era, where leaders and elders gradually assumed more specialized roles in the church. The shift toward hierarchical structures and the clergy/laity distinction became more pronounced as Christianity spread and evolved.

Clericalism: The eventual separation between the clergy and the laity led to certain theological and practical issues. Theological authority and responsibility were often concentrated in the clergy, which some argue was a departure from the early Christian emphasis on shared leadership and ministry.

Protestant Reformation: The Protestant Reformation in the 16th century challenged the existing clergy/laity distinction, emphasizing the priesthood of all believers and promoting congregational involvement in church governance. This movement sought to align with what proponents of the statement see as the biblical model.

Diverse Interpretations:

Variation Among Christian Traditions: It's important to note that the understanding of clergy and the clergy/laity distinction varies among Christian traditions. Some, like Roman Catholicism and Eastern Orthodoxy, have well-established clergy systems. In contrast, many Protestant denominations have diverse approaches, with some embracing a more hierarchical structure and others adhering to a less formalized system.

In conclusion, the statement in question represents a particular perspective within the realm of Christian theology and history. Indeed, the New Testament does not explicitly lay out a detailed blueprint for the modern clergy, and the emergence of the clergy/laity distinction is a historical development. However, it's essential to recognize the diversity of interpretations and practices within Christianity and the nuanced ways in which different traditions have sought to balance biblical principles with the practical needs of their congregations. Ultimately, the question of the clergy's role and the clergy/laity distinction remains a subject of theological debate and ecclesiastical tradition within Christianity.

Jesus clarifies that we are all brothers and sisters in Christ and are not to be called "Rabbi," teacher, father, or any other name that might denote a sense of a hierarchy or place above anyone else. He was referring to himself in this passage, so it is clear in reading that if Jesus, the actual Son of God, doesn't desire a place of superiority, neither should we. Instead, we should humble ourselves to better serve the will of God.

CHAPTER 4:

Redefining Prosperity and Success

True Prosperity: A Journey Beyond Material Accumulation

We can spend a lot of time and energy focusing on the cares of the world, like careers, homes, cars, toys, and stuff, all things that are very temporary and short-lived in the eternal timeline of God. But we feel like it is what we are here to do, right?

But Jesus makes it very clear that these things are not to be our focus; we are to concentrate on the eternal treasures, the kind that truly last. Jesus showed us what it looks like to live this out. Remember, Jesus was here as a human, with the same mind, thoughts, and temptations we have. Yet, he clearly demonstrated how to live out the truth. He also reminds us to seek God first; all things needed will be added unto you. It sounds so simple, right? Well, it is the hardest simple thing to do, but it is where the true riches lie—the riches of the Kingdom of God.

In a world often defined by materialism, where success is measured in monetary terms, exploring alternative perspectives on wealth and prosperity is essential. One of the most profound and enduring teachings on this subject comes from the life and words of Jesus Christ. His message challenges our conventional notions of riches and invites us to consider the profound wealth that resides within the human heart.

The true prosperity Jesus is talking about is not of this world. Instead, it emphasizes putting the focus on the oneness and interconnectedness of us all. It encourages us not to hoard everything for ourselves but to be willing to give up whatever we have for higher prosperity, which is the love and care for our fellow humans. The riches of this world are transient, and we should view them as tools for the higher good of all. This, according to Jesus, is what constitutes TRUE RICHES.

The Counter-Cultural Message

Jesus was a revolutionary figure in many ways, and his teachings on wealth and prosperity were no exception. In a society obsessed with wealth, power, and status, he offered a radically different perspective. Instead of focusing on the accumulation of material possessions, Jesus emphasized the importance of inner wealth, compassion, and spiritual abundance.

One of the most well-known passages in the Bible that illustrates Jesus' perspective on wealth is found in the Gospel of Matthew:

"Do not store up for yourselves treasures on earth, where moth and rust destroy, and where thieves break in and steal. But store up for yourselves treasures in heaven, where neither moth nor rust destroys, and where thieves do not break in or steal. For where your treasure is, there your heart will be also." (Matthew 6:19-21, NIV)

In these verses, Jesus encourages us to shift our focus away from earthly possessions, which are impermanent and subject to loss, and instead invest in spiritual and eternal treasures. He is reminding us that the true measure of prosperity isn't found in our bank accounts or the size of our houses but in the state of our hearts and the quality of our relationships.

The Parable of the Rich Fool

To illustrate his point further, Jesus told a parable about a wealthy man who was solely focused on accumulating more and more wealth. This parable, found in Luke 12:16-21, is a cautionary tale about the dangers of greed and the emptiness of materialism.

In the story, the rich man had an abundant harvest and faced a dilemma of what to do with his surplus. Instead of considering the needs of others or using his wealth for a higher purpose, he decided to build bigger barns to hoard his possessions. He told himself, "You have plenty of grain laid up for many years. Take life easy; eat, drink, and be merry" (Luke 12:19, NIV).

However, God's response to the man's attitude was a stark reminder of the impermanence of earthly riches. "You fool! This very night your life will be demanded from you. Then who will get what you have prepared for yourself?" (Luke 12:20, NIV).

This parable underscores Jesus' message that true prosperity isn't measured by the size of our bank accounts but by the state of our souls. It challenges the notion that accumulating wealth for personal gain is the path to lasting happiness and fulfillment.

The Rich Young Ruler

Another powerful encounter in the Gospels that illustrates Jesus' teachings on wealth is the story of the rich young ruler (Matthew 19:16-30). This young man approached Jesus and asked what he needed to do to inherit eternal life. He claimed to have kept all the commandments from his youth, but he still felt something was missing.

In response, Jesus said, "If you want to be perfect, go, sell your possessions and give to the poor, and you will have treasure in heaven. Then come, follow me" (Matthew 19:21, NIV).

The young man's reaction was one of sadness because he had great wealth and couldn't bear to part with it. Jesus' instruction challenged him to prioritize his spiritual well-being over material possessions. This story highlights the difficulty many people face in detaching themselves from their wealth and the counter-cultural nature of Jesus' message.

The Widow's Mite

In another poignant example, Jesus used a simple act of giving to teach a profound lesson about wealth and generosity. In the Gospel of Mark, Jesus sat near the temple treasury and observed people making their offerings. Many wealthy individuals contributed large sums of money, but a poor widow caught his attention.

Calling his disciples, Jesus said, "Truly I tell you, this poor widow has put more into the treasury than all the others. They all gave out of their wealth, but she, out of her poverty, put in everything—all she had to live on" (Mark 12:43-44, NIV).

In this moment, Jesus highlighted the significance of one's heart and intention in giving. The widow's meager gift, though small in monetary value, held greater spiritual value because it represented her complete trust in God and her willingness to give sacrificially. Her example challenges us to reevaluate our understanding of prosperity and recognize the true wealth that comes from a generous and selfless heart.

The Kingdom of God

Throughout his ministry, Jesus often spoke of the "Kingdom of God" or the "Kingdom of Heaven." This concept was central to his teachings on prosperity and success. In the Gospel of Matthew, Jesus compares the Kingdom of Heaven to a treasure hidden in a field, saying that "when a man found it, he hid it again, and then in his joy went and sold all he had and bought that field" (Matthew

13:44, NIV).

This parable illustrates that the Kingdom of God is of such incomparable value that it is worth sacrificing everything else to attain it. Jesus taught that the truest form of prosperity is found in aligning our lives with God's kingdom, which is characterized by righteousness, love, and peace.

Lessons for Redefining Prosperity

The teachings of Jesus on wealth and prosperity provide profound lessons for those seeking to redefine success in a materialistic world. Here are some key takeaways:

Prioritize Spiritual Wealth: Jesus reminds us that material possessions are temporary and can be lost or stolen. Instead of pursuing wealth for its own sake, we should prioritize the development of inner qualities like love, compassion, and humility.

Generosity and Sacrifice: The stories of the rich young ruler and the widow's mite emphasize the importance of generosity and sacrificial giving. True prosperity is not about hoarding wealth but about using it to make a positive impact on the lives of others.

Detachment from Materialism: Jesus challenges us to break free from the grip of materialism. While everyone doesn't need to sell all their possessions, we should be willing to let go of anything that hinders our spiritual growth or blinds us to the needs of others.

The Kingdom of God:

Success, according to Jesus, is ultimately about entering into a deep and transformative relationship with God and participating in the values of God's kingdom. This involves seeking righteousness, peace, and justice in all aspects of our lives.

Eternal Perspective:

Jesus' teachings invite us to adopt an eternal perspective. Instead of being solely concerned with our earthly lives, we should consider the long-term impact of our actions and decisions on our spiritual well-being and relationship with God.

In a world that often equates prosperity with financial wealth, Jesus' countercultural message challenges us to redefine our priorities and values. It encourages us to recognize that true riches are found in the condition of our hearts, our relationships with others, and our alignment with the values of God's kingdom.

Modern-day Applications

Embracing a perspective of prosperity and success that goes beyond material accumulation aligns with many principles found in the teachings of Jesus. Here's a practical list of modern-day applications for followers of Jesus to redefine their true prosperity and success:

Generosity and Philanthropy:

- Contribute to charitable causes and organizations that focus on helping the less fortunate.
- Volunteer time and skills to support community projects and initiatives.

Building Meaningful Relationships:

- Prioritize building and maintaining strong, positive relationships with family, friends, and the community.
- Invest time in nurturing emotional and spiritual connections.

Spiritual Growth and Mindfulness:

- Engage in regular prayer, meditation, or other spiritual practices to deepen your relationship with God.
- Cultivate mindfulness and gratitude in daily life, appreciating the present moment.

Acts of Kindness:

- Look for opportunities to perform random acts of kindness for others without expecting anything in return.
- Practice forgiveness and reconciliation in relationships.

Personal Development:

- Focus on continual self-improvement and learning, aligning personal goals with spiritual values.
- Develop and use your talents and abilities to positively impact the lives of others.

Environmental Stewardship:

- Adopt sustainable practices in daily living to care for the environment.
- Support initiatives that promote environmental conservation and responsible resource use.

Health and Well-being:

- Prioritize physical and mental well-being, recognizing the body as a temple.
- Encourage healthy lifestyle choices and support others in their health journeys.

Advocacy for Justice and Equality:

- Stand up against injustice, discrimination, and inequality.
- Advocate for policies and practices that promote fairness, compassion, and the well-being of all.

Contentment and Gratitude:

- Practice contentment with what you have, expressing gratitude for life's blessings.
- Avoid excessive consumerism and the pursuit of material possessions as a source of fulfillment.

Community Involvement:

- Engage actively in your local community, participating in initiatives that enhance the well-being of all community members.
- Foster a sense of belonging and inclusivity within your community.

Balanced Work-Life Integration:

- Strive for a healthy balance between work and personal life, avoiding the trap of overwork.
- Prioritize time for rest, reflection, and spending quality time with loved ones.

Cultivating Joy and Inner Peace:

- Seek joy and inner peace through spiritual practices, positive relationships, and a purposeful life.
- Let go of stress and anxiety by trusting God's plan and embracing a positive outlook.

Redefining prosperity and success in these ways aligns with the teachings of Jesus, emphasizing love, compassion, and service to others over the accumulation of material wealth.

Food for Soulful Consideration - Moralism is based on the law; the Gospel is based on grace.

The statement, "Those preaching moralism are preaching a message contrary to the Gospel. Moralism is based on the law; the Gospel is based on grace. Moralism is a false gospel, which is really no gospel at all," reflects a theological perspective that is deeply rooted in Christian tradition and biblical teaching. To provide a commentary on this statement, we can examine the biblical and non-biblical historical context.

Biblical Perspective:

The Bible, particularly the New Testament, emphasizes the distinction between moralism and the Gospel of grace. Moralism, in this context, refers to a strict adherence to a moral code or the belief that salvation can be earned through good deeds and obedience to the law. This perspective is often associated with the Pharisees and religious leaders of Jesus's time. Conversely, the Gospel centers on the belief that salvation is a gift from God, offered through faith in Jesus Christ.

Law vs. Grace: The Bible clearly distinguishes between living under the law and living under grace. The law, as given in the Old Testament, was meant to reveal humanity's need for a Savior and to set standards for righteous living. However, the Gospel reveals that no one can perfectly fulfill the law. Thus, salvation comes through God's grace, not human effort.

Legalism and Pharisaism: The New Testament contains numerous passages where Jesus criticized the Pharisees and teachers of the law for their emphasis on outward morality and strict adherence to rules while neglecting matters of the heart (Matthew 23:23-28). This is a classic example of moralism being at odds with the Gospel's message of repentance, forgiveness, and grace.

Salvation by Faith: The Apostle Paul, in his letters, notably underscores that salvation comes through faith in Christ, not by works of the law (Ephesians 2:8-9). This grace-based message is a cornerstone of Christian theology.

Historical Perspective:

Throughout Christian history, debates and theological discussions have centered on balancing moralism and grace. The early church grappled with issues related to legalism and the role of good works in salvation. In some periods, moralism dominated Christian thinking, leading to practices such as indulgences in the medieval Catholic Church, which were challenged by the Protestant Reformation.

Reformation: The Protestant Reformation, led by figures like Martin Luther and John Calvin, emphasized the primacy of grace in salvation and rejected the legalistic practices of the medieval church. This movement played a significant role in shaping modern Christian theology.

Christian Denominations: Various Christian denominations and traditions have different perspectives on the relationship between moralism and grace. Some may place more emphasis on personal righteousness and adherence to moral codes. In contrast, others emphasize the sufficiency of God's grace for salvation.

In conclusion, the statement that preaching moralism contradicts the Gospel is firmly rooted in biblical teaching and has historical relevance in Christian theology. The central message of the Gospel is that salvation is a gift of grace, not something earned through strict adherence to moral laws. While moral living is encouraged in Christianity, it is not how one attains salvation. This perspective reflects a core theological principle in Christianity that continues to shape the beliefs and practices of Christians today.

I've observed that within the framework of organized Christian religion, there is often a significant emphasis on the moral aspect—showcasing a 'look at me, I am good, and you are bad' mentality. There's a desire to fix those we perceive as worse off than ourselves, leading to what I call a 'spiritual ego.' Instead of focusing on the love and grace given to us and extending that same love and grace to others, the emphasis tends to shift. Religions often take root because our minds are preoccupied with notions of 'good and evil,' essentially playing the role of God. This strays from the essence of truly giving, sharing, and living out God's gracious love—the ideals Jesus wanted us to embody.

CHAPTER 5:

A Gospel of Inclusion and Acceptance

Beyond Boundaries: Building a Diverse
and All-Inclusive Community

I asked AI to "Write a story based on what we know about Jesus Christ and how he would want us to relate to the LGBTQ community and the issues within our country? Tell the story as a true life that could have been the reality as he would have answered."

In a small, sunlit village nestled between rolling hills, there lived a humble carpenter named Joseph. He was known for his kindness and compassion, traits he believed he had learned from the teachings of his dear friend and spiritual guide, Jesus of Nazareth.

One warm afternoon, Joseph was in his workshop, meticulously crafting a piece of furniture, when he heard a soft knock at his door. He opened it to find a young man named Benjamin standing there, tears glistening in his eyes.

"Joseph," Benjamin began, his voice trembling, "I need your help. I have something important to tell you."

Joseph welcomed Benjamin inside, sensing the urgency in his tone. As they sat down, Benjamin took a deep breath and said, "I need to share something with you. I'm gay, Joseph."

Joseph looked at Benjamin with the same warmth and love he had seen in the eyes of Jesus. He reached out and gently placed a hand on Benjamin's shoulder, saying, "Benjamin, I am honored that you trust me enough to share this with me. Remember this, my friend, you are a child of God, and His love knows no boundaries. Jesus taught us to love one another unconditionally. I will always stand by you, just as I believe He would."

Tears welled up in Benjamin's eyes as he felt a weight lifted off his chest. He had been afraid to confide in anyone, fearing rejection or judgment, but Joseph's acceptance and love gave him hope.

Over time, Joseph and Benjamin became closer than ever. They often discussed Jesus' teachings and how they could apply them to their lives. Together, they realized that Jesus' message was one of love, acceptance, and compassion for all.

Word of their friendship and Joseph's unwavering support for Benjamin spread throughout the village. Some people questioned Joseph's actions, but he remained steadfast in his belief that he was following the path of love as Jesus had taught.

One day, a gathering was held in the village square to address a divisive issue plaguing their community. There had been growing tension and animosity between different groups, each holding strongly to their beliefs. Joseph and Benjamin attended the meeting, hoping to make a difference.

In the annals of human history, few figures have left as indelible a mark as Jesus of Nazareth. His life and teachings have reverberated through time and continue to shape the beliefs and values of billions around the world. At the heart of Jesus' message lies a gospel of inclusion and acceptance, a revolutionary call to break down barriers and embrace the marginalized.

Throughout his ministry, Jesus demonstrated a radical approach to inclusivity, challenging the norms and prejudices of his time. In this chapter, we will explore the stories and teachings that exemplify his commitment to welcoming all into the fold, particularly those on the fringes of society.

The Outcasts and the Welcome Table

One of the most poignant aspects of Jesus' ministry was his willingness to engage with those society had cast aside. In a time when lepers were shunned, tax collectors were despised, and the physically impaired were often considered cursed, Jesus saw beyond these societal labels. He saw the inherent worth and dignity in every individual, regardless of their station in life.

The story of Zacchaeus, the tax collector, is a prime example of Jesus' radical embrace of the marginalized. Tax collectors in ancient Israel were not only seen as collaborators with the Roman oppressors but were also notorious for their corruption and exploitation of their fellow citizens. When Jesus saw Zacchaeus perched in a tree, he didn't scold or condemn him; instead, he invited himself to Zacchaeus' home for a meal. This act of reaching out to a tax collector sent shockwaves through the community, challenging their preconceived notions of who was deserving of grace and acceptance.

Similarly, Jesus' interaction with the Samaritan woman at the well-challenged cultural and religious boundaries. Jews and Samaritans were bitter rivals and a Jewish man talking to a Samaritan woman was highly unusual. Yet, Jesus not only engaged in conversation with her but also revealed his true identity as the Messiah. This encounter demonstrated that the gospel of inclusion transcended ethnic and gender divisions, emphasizing the importance of spiritual connection over cultural barriers.

Healing and Restoration

Jesus' ministry was marked by countless acts of healing and restoration, many of which focused on those marginalized due to physical or mental conditions. In the ancient world, illness and disability often carried a heavy social stigma. People with leprosy were considered unclean and were ostracized from their communities. Those afflicted with mental illness were often labeled as possessed by evil spirits.

However, Jesus saw beyond these afflictions and treated individuals with compassion and dignity. He healed lepers, restored sight to the blind, and cast out demons, not as mere displays of power but as profound demonstrations of his love and acceptance for those whom society had rejected.

The story of the man born blind in John 9 is a compelling illustration of Jesus' healing ministry. The man's condition had caused him a lifetime of suffering and exclusion. When Jesus encountered him, he didn't offer platitudes or assign blame for the man's affliction. Instead, he healed him and restored not only his physical sight but also his place within the community.

By breaking down the barriers of illness and disability, Jesus not only showcased his divine power but also emphasized the intrinsic worth of every individual, regardless of their physical or mental condition.

The Parable of the Good Samaritan

Perhaps one of the most famous stories that embodies Jesus' message of inclusion is the Parable of the Good Samaritan. In response to a question about who one's neighbor is, Jesus tells the story of a man who is beaten, robbed, and left for dead on the side of the road. Several religious figures pass by the wounded man. But it is a Samaritan, someone from a despised ethnic group, who stops to care for him.

This parable challenges us to broaden our understanding of who our neighbors are and what it means to love them. Jesus' choice of a Samaritan as the hero of the story shocks his audience, forcing them to confront their prejudices and biases. He teaches that our love and compassion should extend beyond our communities and even to those we might consider enemies or outsiders.

The Parable of the Good Samaritan encapsulates the essence of Jesus' gospel of inclusion—a call to break down barriers, see the humanity in all people, and extend love and compassion without discrimination.

The Woman Caught in Adultery

Another powerful story of Jesus' radical embrace of the marginalized is the encounter with the woman caught in adultery. In this narrative found in John 8, religious leaders bring a woman they claim was caught in the act of adultery and demand that she be stoned, as was the custom of the time. Jesus responds with a challenge: "Let any one of you who is without sin be the first to throw a stone at her."

This simple but profound statement exposes the hypocrisy of the accusers and reminds us all of our own imperfections. Jesus refuses to condemn the woman and offers her forgiveness and a fresh start. This act of mercy stands as a powerful reminder that judgment and condemnation have no place in the gospel of inclusion and acceptance.

Lessons from the Margins

As we delve into these stories from the life of Jesus, we begin to see a pattern of radical inclusivity and acceptance that challenges the boundaries and prejudices of his time—and of our own. But what do these lessons from the margins mean for us today? How can we embody the gospel of inclusion in our lives and communities?

1. Recognize our biases: The first step toward embracing the marginalized is acknowledging our biases and prejudices. Just as the religious leaders in the story of the woman caught in adultery had to confront their own imperfections, we must be willing to examine our hearts and minds for any preconceived notions that hinder our ability to welcome all.

2. Engage with empathy: Jesus didn't just preach inclusivity; he engaged with people on a personal level. We, too, must be willing to step out of our comfort zones and engage with those different from us. It's through personal connections that we can truly understand the experiences and struggles of others.

3. Challenge societal norms: The gospel of inclusion often challenges the status quo. It requires us to question the norms and structures perpetuating exclusion and inequality. Just as Jesus challenged the religious authorities of his time, we must be willing to challenge systems that marginalize people based on their race, gender, sexuality, or any other characteristic.

4. Extend grace and forgiveness: Jesus' response to the woman caught in adultery teaches us the power of forgiveness and second chances. In our interactions with others, we should seek opportunities for reconciliation and restoration rather than condemnation.

5. Advocate for justice: Jesus' message of inclusion was not passive. He actively sought justice for the marginalized. We, too, must be advocates for social and economic justice, working to dismantle systems of oppression that keep people on the margins.

6. Create inclusive communities: Building on Jesus' example, we should strive to create communities that reflect the gospel of inclusion. This means intentionally welcoming people from all walks of life, valuing diversity, and ensuring no one feels excluded or unworthy.

Beyond Boundaries: Building a Diverse and All-Inclusive Community

In the previous chapter, we explored the life and teachings of Jesus, which exemplify a gospel of inclusion and acceptance. Now, we focus on the practical aspects of living out this gospel in our lives and communities. How can we go beyond the boundaries that separate us and build diverse and all-inclusive communities that mirror Jesus' radical embrace of the marginalized?

The Power of Diversity

Diversity is a cornerstone of an all-inclusive community. Just as Jesus welcomed people from all walks of life, we, too, should embrace diversity in our communities. Diversity encompasses a wide range of differences, including but not limited to:

- Cultural diversity: Embracing people from various cultural backgrounds, ethnicities, and traditions.

- Racial diversity: Recognizing and valuing people of different races and ethnicities.

- Gender diversity: Affirming the identities and experiences of people of all gender identities.

- Sexual orientation diversity: Welcoming individuals of diverse sexual orientations and identities.

- Economic diversity: Ensuring that people from different economic backgrounds have equal access and opportunities.

- Ability diversity: Creating spaces that are accessible and inclusive for people with disabilities.

- Religious diversity: Respecting and learning from people of various faith traditions or belief systems.

Diverse communities are not only more reflective of the broader world but also offer a rich tapestry of perspectives, experiences, and talents. This diversity can lead to greater creativity, innovation, and problem-solving as people bring unique insights to the table.

Fostering Inclusivity

Building an all-inclusive community goes beyond merely having diversity. It requires actively fostering an inclusive environment where all members feel welcomed, valued, and respected. Here are some key principles to consider:

1. Open and respectful dialogue: Encourage open and respectful communication among community members. Create spaces where people can share their thoughts, experiences, and concerns without fear of judgment.

2. Education and awareness: Promote education and awareness about different aspects of diversity. This can include workshops, seminars, or guest speakers who can help community members learn about and appreciate various perspectives.

3. Representation: Ensure all voices are heard and represented in decision-making processes. This may involve diverse leadership and committees that actively seek input from all community members.

4. Accessible spaces: Make physical and digital spaces accessible to everyone, including those with disabilities. Ensure that meetings, events, and materials are designed with accessibility in mind.

5. Zero tolerance for discrimination: Clearly communicate a zero-tolerance policy for discrimination, harassment, or exclusion based on any aspect of diversity. Enforce these policies consistently.

Overcoming Challenges

Building an all-inclusive community is not without its challenges. Resistance to change, unconscious biases, and fear of the unknown can all hinder progress. Here are some strategies to overcome these challenges:

1. Engage in dialogue: Encourage open and non-judgmental dialogue about concerns and fears related to diversity and inclusion. Creating a safe space for such conversations can help address misunderstandings and build empathy.

2. Lead by example: Community leaders and influencers play a crucial role in setting the tone for inclusivity. Lead by example and demonstrate your commitment to diversity and inclusion through your actions and decisions.

3. Offer training and resources: Provide resources and training to help community members understand and address unconscious biases. This can lead to greater awareness and more inclusive behaviors.

4. Listen and learn: Be open to feedback from community members who may have experienced exclusion or discrimination. Learn from their experiences and use their input to make improvements.

5. Stay committed: Building an all-inclusive community is an ongoing process. Stay committed to the journey, even when faced with challenges or setbacks. Recognize that progress may take time.

The Role of Faith Communities

Faith communities, in particular, have a unique opportunity to lead by example when it comes to building diverse and all-inclusive communities. Many religious traditions share common values of love, compassion, and acceptance. Here are some ways faith communities can play a pivotal role:

1. Interfaith dialogue: Engage in interfaith dialogue to build bridges of understanding and cooperation between different faith traditions. Promote mutual respect and collaboration on issues of common concern.

2. Social justice advocacy: Advocate for social justice and equity within your faith community and broader society. Take a stand on issues related to discrimination, poverty, and inequality.

3. Community outreach: Extend a welcoming hand to those on the margins of society. This may include providing resources for the homeless, supporting refugees, or advocating for the rights of LGBTQ+ individuals.

4. Inclusive worship: Ensure that your worship services and religious activities are inclusive and accessible to all. This includes considering the needs of people with disabilities and creating a welcoming atmosphere for people of all backgrounds.

5. Education and awareness: Use your faith community as a platform for education and awareness about diversity and inclusion. Host seminars, workshops, and discussions on relevant topics.

Conclusion

Building a diverse and all-inclusive community is a noble goal and a reflection of the gospel of inclusion and acceptance that Jesus preached and embodied. It requires deliberate effort, ongoing commitment, and a willingness to challenge the boundaries that divide us. By fostering diversity and inclusivity, we can create communities that mirror the radical embrace of the marginalized Jesus exemplified in his life and teachings.

As we explore a gospel of inclusion and acceptance, we will continue to delve into practical strategies, real-world examples, and inspiring stories that illustrate how individuals and communities are working to break down barriers and build a more inclusive world.

Modern Day Applications

Embracing a Gospel of Inclusion and Acceptance involves adopting attitudes and behaviors that promote unity and understanding among diverse individuals. Here's a list of practical actions and behaviors that a follower of Jesus can consider:

Practice Unconditional Love:

Love others without judgment or discrimination, just as Jesus loved unconditionally.

Listen Actively:

Seek to understand others by listening attentively and empathetically to their experiences and perspectives.

Cultivate Humility:

Approach others with humility, recognizing that everyone has unique gifts, experiences, and insights to offer.

Challenge Stereotypes:

Avoid making assumptions about people based on stereotypes and actively challenge prejudiced attitudes.

Promote Inclusivity in Church Activities:

Ensure that church events and activities are welcoming and inclusive to people of all backgrounds, races, genders, and socioeconomic statuses.

Educate Yourself:

Take the initiative to learn about different cultures, religions, and backgrounds to better understand and appreciate diversity.

Advocate for Social Justice:

Stand up for justice and equality, advocating for policies and practices that promote fairness and inclusivity in society.

Engage in Interfaith Dialogue:

Foster understanding and dialogue with individuals from different faith traditions to build bridges and promote mutual respect.

Celebrate Diversity:

Acknowledge and celebrate the diverse gifts and talents that each person brings to the community.

Address Implicit Bias:

Reflect on and address any unconscious biases you may have, working toward a more open and accepting mindset.

Create a Welcoming Environment:

Ensure that your church or community space is physically and emotionally welcoming to everyone.

Extend Acts of Kindness:

Perform acts of kindness and service to others without regard to their background, fostering a spirit of generosity and compassion.

Build Cross-Cultural Relationships:

Intentionally build relationships with people from different cultural backgrounds, fostering understanding and friendship.

Promote Diversity in Leadership:

Encourage and support the involvement of individuals from diverse backgrounds in leadership roles within the church community.

Pray for Unity:

Pray for unity and understanding within your community and for a world that embraces the principles of inclusion and acceptance.

Remember that embodying a Gospel of Inclusion and Acceptance is an ongoing process involving a commitment to continuous growth and openness to others.

Food for Soulful Consideration - Politics is a carnal pursuit

The statement, "Politics is a carnal pursuit that can distract Christians from their calling, darken their spiritual vision, and weaken their faith," reflects a perspective on the intersection of religion and politics debated throughout history. It draws from both biblical and non-biblical historical facts to support its claims. Let's delve into these arguments:

Biblical Perspective:

Distraction from Calling: The Bible emphasizes the importance of Christians living out their faith and fulfilling their calling to spread the Gospel and love their neighbors. Engaging in politics can sometimes lead to distractions from this spiritual calling. In the New Testament, Jesus instructed his followers to be "in the world, but not of the world." Political involvement can often lead to worldly preoccupations that may divert attention from one's spiritual mission.

Darkening of Spiritual Vision: The Bible warns against the love of power and wealth, both of which can be intertwined with politics. In Matthew 6:24, Jesus warns, "No one can serve two masters. Either you will hate the one and love the other, or you will be devoted to the one and despise the other." Becoming entangled in the political power struggle may lead to a distortion of one's spiritual vision as one becomes consumed by worldly concerns.

Weakening of Faith: Politics can be a contentious and divisive arena. Engaging in political debates and battles can sometimes erode the unity and love that Christians are called to uphold. In the Epistles, we find numerous references to maintaining the "unity of the Spirit" and striving for peace. Involvement in politics can, at times, result in a weakening of one's faith, as the pursuit of power and ideological conflict can undermine the core principles of Christianity.

Non-Biblical Historical Perspective:

Historical Precedents: Throughout history, there have been instances where the intertwining of politics and religion has led to conflict, persecution, and corruption. The Crusades, the Inquisition, and various religious wars serve as non-biblical examples of how political power can corrupt the spiritual message of Christianity and lead to violence and oppression.

Moral and Ethical Compromises: Engaging in politics often requires making difficult moral and ethical compromises. These compromises can test the core values of a Christian's faith, leading to moral dilemmas that may challenge one's spirituality. Historically, politicians have sometimes had to compromise their principles for political gain, which can be a stumbling block for Christians seeking to live by a higher moral code.

Idolization of Political Leaders: Political leaders are often held up as heroes or saviors, and their actions are closely tied to a nation's well-being. This can sometimes border on the veneration of political figures, which is contrary to Christian principles of worshiping God alone. This historical tendency to idolize political leaders highlights how politics can be a potential threat to a Christian's faith.

The statement that politics is a carnal pursuit that can distract Christians from their calling, darken their spiritual vision, and weaken their faith finds support in both biblical teachings and non-biblical historical examples. However, it's essential to acknowledge that not all Christians view political engagement in the same way. Many believe that political involvement can also be a means to fulfill their calling by advocating for justice, mercy, and compassion. The relationship between faith and politics is complex and varies among individuals and communities. However, these concerns remain important aspects to consider in the ongoing dialogue surrounding the role of Christianity in political life.

In conclusion, as I delve deeper into my understanding of Jesus, I find that it's not something we should primarily focus on as followers of Jesus. He explicitly states, "My kingdom is not of this realm," and emphasizes rendering unto Caesar what is Caesar's, among many other points in the Bible. Jesus advocates for loving one another, and it becomes challenging to truly love our fellow humans when our focus is on being right, proving our points, or engaging in political battles for or against various causes. This tendency reflects our inclination to play God for others rather than simply embracing and loving them. Our desire to fix others can hinder the genuine love Jesus encourages us to embody.

CHAPTER 6:

Nonviolence in a Violent World

Transformative Justice:
How Nonviolence Creates Lasting Change

I asked AI to write a perspective on the Complex and enduring conflict in the Middle East between Israel and Palestine. It came up with this, and it's very much on point with the message of nonviolence in a violent world, the message of Jesus!

The complex and enduring conflict in the Middle East between Israel and Palestine carries a deep historical and religious significance that resonates with both biblical and non-biblical narratives. To comprehend this multifaceted issue, one must explore its historical roots and religious ties and consider what messages of peace and reconciliation can be drawn from the life and teachings of Jesus Christ.

Historically, the Israel-Palestine conflict has its origins in the late 19th and early 20th centuries, intertwined with the legacy of colonialism, the fall of the Ottoman Empire, and the establishment of the State of Israel in 1948. It involves territorial disputes, competing claims, and deep-seated historical grievances that date back centuries. The region is a cradle of civilization, with a rich tapestry of cultures, religions, and identities.

From a biblical perspective, the region holds deep religious significance for Jews, Christians, and Muslims. It is the land of the Bible, the birthplace of Judaism and Christianity, and the third holiest site in Islam. The biblical narratives, particularly in the Old Testament, are intertwined with the land, and the promise of a homeland for the Jewish people is central to these texts. The New Testament, meanwhile, promotes values of love, compassion, and reconciliation, exemplified by Jesus Christ.

In this context, it is instructive to consider what Jesus Christ might say in response to the ongoing conflict. He would likely emphasize the principles of love, forgiveness, and reconciliation, as found in his teachings. His famous Sermon on the Mount includes the call for peacemakers to be blessed, and he encouraged his followers to love their enemies.

From a Christian perspective, Jesus' teachings underscore the importance of empathy, compassion, and seeking peaceful solutions. He would likely advocate for dialogue, understanding, and reconciliation between Israelis and Palestinians. He might remind us of the story of the Good Samaritan, illustrating the need to extend compassion to those who are different or perceived as enemies.

While acknowledging the deep historical and religious roots of the conflict, it is crucial to remember that peacemaking requires recognizing humanity and suffering on both sides. A perspective rooted in the spirit of Christ's message could encourage constructive dialogue, cooperation, and the pursuit of peace that "passes all understanding."

The path to peace in the Middle East is fraught with challenges, but it is not an impossible endeavor. By drawing inspiration from the teachings of Jesus Christ, along with principles of justice, human rights, and international cooperation, a resolution that respects the rights and dignity of both Israelis and Palestinians can be sought. Such a peace would honor the historical and religious legacies of the region while promoting a better future for all who call it home. It is a call to rise above division and animosity, seek common ground, and work toward a peace that embodies the highest ideals of compassion, understanding, and reconciliation.

I personally find that AI is doing a better job of understanding the truth of JESUS' RED LETTER messages because it doesn't have an emotional story or knowledge of good and evil to cloud the teachings and words of JESUS. It simply sees JESUS as JESUS is and gives us the truth of the message, not based on emotions but simple facts.

In a world often marred by violence and conflict, the concept of nonviolence stands as a beacon of hope and a powerful force for change. Throughout history, many individuals and movements have embraced nonviolence as a means to address social, political, and moral issues. One of the most influential figures in this regard is Jesus of Nazareth, whose teachings and actions have left an indelible mark on the philosophy of nonviolence.

The Life and Teachings of Jesus

Jesus, a central figure in Christianity, lived in a turbulent period of history characterized by Roman occupation, social unrest, and religious divisions. His life and teachings, recorded in the New Testament of the Bible, have profoundly impacted the world for over two millennia.

At the heart of Jesus' message was the principle of love and nonviolence. He taught his followers to "turn the other cheek" when faced with aggression, to "love your enemies," and to "bless those who curse you." These teachings challenged the prevailing norms of his time and continue to challenge us today.

The Courage to Stand Against Violence

One of the most iconic stories illustrating Jesus' commitment to nonviolence is the incident in the Garden of Gethsemane. On the night before his crucifixion, Jesus faced an imminent arrest by Roman authorities. His disciples, filled with fear and desperation, wanted to defend him with violence. But Jesus, with unwavering courage, stopped them and said, "Put your sword back into its place; for all who take the sword will perish by the sword" (Matthew 26:52).

This powerful statement encapsulates the essence of Jesus' pacifism. He recognized that violence begets violence, and he chose a path of nonresistance even in the face of grave danger. Jesus' willingness to embrace suffering rather than inflict harm demonstrated a profound commitment to nonviolence.

The Legacy of Jesus' Nonviolence

The legacy of Jesus' nonviolence extends far beyond his own time. His teachings have inspired countless individuals and movements throughout history, from Mahatma Gandhi to Martin Luther King Jr. These leaders recognized the moral strength of nonviolence and its capacity to bring about profound social and political change.

Gandhi, often referred to as the "apostle of nonviolence," drew heavily from Jesus' teachings in his struggle for Indian independence from British rule. He believed that nonviolence was not a sign of weakness but a manifestation of inner strength. Gandhi's commitment to peaceful resistance ultimately led to India's independence in 1947 and left an enduring legacy for future generations.

Martin Luther King Jr., another champion of nonviolence, was deeply influenced by Gandhi's philosophy and Jesus' teachings. In the American civil rights movement, King and his followers employed nonviolent resistance tactics such as sit-ins, boycotts, and peaceful marches. Their commitment to nonviolence played a pivotal role in dismantling racial segregation and advancing civil rights in the United States.

Challenges and Misinterpretations

While Jesus' message of nonviolence is powerful, it has not been without challenges and misinterpretations. Some critics argue that his teachings are unrealistic and impractical in a world rife with violence and conflict. They contend that nonviolence can be passive and ineffective in the face of ruthless aggressors.

However, proponents of nonviolence assert that its power lies not in passivity but in active resistance. Nonviolent movements often require immense courage, sacrifice, and strategic planning. They aim to expose the injustice and brutality of oppressive systems, thereby gaining public sympathy and support.

Furthermore, nonviolence is not a one-size-fits-all approach. It requires adaptability and creativity in different contexts. What works in one situation may not work in another, and the success of nonviolent movements often depends on a deep understanding of the specific circumstances at hand.

The Limitations of Retributive Justice

Traditional approaches to justice, often characterized as retributive, focus on punishing wrongdoers as a means of redressing harm. While retributive justice may offer a sense of closure for victims and society, it has several limitations:

Perpetuating Cycles of Violence: Retributive justice can perpetuate cycles of violence, as punitive measures often lead to anger, resentment, and a desire for revenge. This can result in a never-ending cycle of harm.

Ignoring Root Causes: Retributive justice tends to overlook the underlying factors that contribute to criminal behavior, such as poverty, trauma, and systemic inequalities. By merely punishing individuals, it fails to address the root causes of crime.

Focusing on Individual Accountability: Retributive justice places primary emphasis on holding individuals accountable for their actions, sometimes neglecting the broader social context that may have contributed to their wrongdoing.

The Emergence of Transformative Justice

In response to the shortcomings of retributive justice, transformative justice has gained prominence as an alternative approach. Transformative justice seeks to transform individuals, communities, and systems in the aftermath of harm. It is rooted in principles of nonviolence, empathy, and accountability.

Key principles of transformative justice include:

Healing and Restoration: Instead of punishment, transformative justice prioritizes the healing and restoration of all parties involved in a harmful incident. This includes the victim, the offender, and the community.

Community Involvement: Transformative justice encourages the active involvement of the affected community in the resolution process. This community-based approach fosters empathy, understanding, and support.

Addressing Root Causes: Transformative justice acknowledges that harm often results from systemic issues such as poverty, racism, and inequality. It seeks to address these root causes to prevent future harm.

Accountability and Learning: Offenders are held accountable for their actions but in a way that encourages personal growth and learning. This accountability is not punitive but transformative.

Nonviolence as the Foundation of Transformative Justice

At the core of transformative justice is the principle of nonviolence. This principle asserts that violence, whether physical or punitive, only begets more violence. Nonviolence recognizes the humanity in all individuals and seeks to resolve conflicts without causing further harm.

The connection between nonviolence and transformative justice is profound:

Breaking the Cycle of Harm: Transformative justice aims to break the cycle of harm by rejecting punitive measures and focusing on healing and reconciliation. This aligns with the nonviolent principle of refusing to respond to violence with violence.

Restoring Dignity: Nonviolence upholds the inherent dignity

of all individuals, including those who have caused harm. Transformative justice similarly seeks to restore the dignity of both victims and offenders through a process of accountability and healing.

Community Building: Both nonviolence and transformative justice emphasize the importance of community. Nonviolence encourages the creation of inclusive and empathetic communities, while transformative justice relies on community involvement in the resolution process.

Addressing Systemic Injustices: Transformative justice recognizes that harm is often a result of systemic injustices. Nonviolence encourages individuals and communities to confront and address these systemic issues peacefully.

Case Studies in Transformative Justice

Transformative justice is not merely a theoretical concept; it has been put into practice in various contexts around the world. Two notable examples highlight the potential of transformative justice to create lasting change:

Restorative Justice in Schools: Restorative justice practices have been increasingly adopted in educational settings. Instead of resorting to punitive measures like suspension, restorative justice involves bringing together the individuals affected by a conflict to engage in dialogue and find mutually agreeable resolutions. This approach not only addresses immediate conflicts but also fosters a culture of empathy and conflict resolution within schools.

Truth and Reconciliation Commissions: Truth and Reconciliation Commissions (TRCs) have been established in countries such as South Africa, Canada, and Rwanda to address historical injustices, including apartheid and genocides. TRCs provide a platform for victims and perpetrators to share their experiences, acknowledge the truth, and work toward reconciliation. While not without challenges, TRCs have contributed to national healing and the prevention of future conflicts.

Challenges and Criticisms

Transformative justice is not without its challenges and criticisms. Some argue that it may not be suitable for all situations, particularly those involving extreme violence or terrorism. Others contend that it places an undue burden on victims to engage in a process of reconciliation with their offenders.

However, proponents of transformative justice argue that its principles can be adapted to a wide range of contexts. They emphasize the importance of voluntary participation and recognize that in cases of severe violence, punitive measures may still be necessary to protect society. Nevertheless, the overarching goal remains the transformation of individuals and communities to prevent future harm.

The Path Forward

Transformative justice, rooted in the principles of nonviolence, offers a path forward in a world where traditional approaches to justice often fall short. By prioritizing healing, restoration, and addressing systemic issues, transformative justice seeks to create a more just and equitable society.

As individuals and communities grapple with the challenges of our time, embracing the principles of nonviolence and transformative justice can lead to meaningful change. It requires a commitment to empathy, dialogue, and accountability, with the understanding that true justice is not merely punitive but transformative—a justice that heals, restores, and ultimately transforms individuals and societies for the better.

In a world marred by violence, the pursuit of nonviolence and transformative justice stands as a beacon of hope, offering a path toward lasting change and a more just and compassionate society.

In this chapter, we have explored the courage of pacifism exemplified by Jesus' stand against violence and the principles of transformative justice rooted in nonviolence. Together, they offer a powerful framework for addressing the complex challenges of a violent world and creating lasting change. These principles invite us to embrace empathy, healing, and reconciliation as essential tools in our quest for a more just and peaceful future.

Modern-day Applications

The courage of pacifism, as exemplified by Jesus' stand against violence, offers valuable lessons for today's world. In a global landscape marked by conflicts, terrorism, and political polarization, the principles of nonviolence can serve as a guiding light for individuals and societies seeking lasting solutions to their problems.

Breaking the Cycle of Violence: Jesus' admonition that "all who take the sword will perish by the sword" reminds us of the cyclical nature of violence. Retaliation often leads to more violence, perpetuating a never-ending cycle of harm. Nonviolence provides a way out of this destructive cycle by offering an alternative to revenge and retribution.

Building Empathy and Understanding: Nonviolent resistance forces us to engage with our adversaries on a human level. By refusing to meet violence with violence, we create opportunities for dialogue and reconciliation. This can lead to a deeper understanding of the root causes of conflict and pave the way for peaceful solutions.

Moral Leadership: Leaders who embrace nonviolence often become symbols of moral courage. Their actions inspire others to join the cause and stand up against injustice. In an age where strong moral leadership is needed more than ever, the example of Jesus and other proponents of nonviolence offers a compelling model.

Effective Social Change: History has shown that nonviolent movements can effectively achieve social and political change. From the civil rights movement in the United States to the anti-apartheid struggle in South Africa, nonviolent resistance has toppled oppressive regimes and dismantled discriminatory systems.

Promoting Human Dignity: Nonviolence upholds the inherent dignity of every human being. It recognizes that even those who commit acts of violence are ultimately deserving of respect and compassion. By refusing to dehumanize our adversaries, we uphold the principle that all individuals have the potential for redemption and transformation.

In a world grappling with pressing issues such as climate change, inequality, and political instability, the courage of pacifism provides a compelling alternative to violence as a means of addressing these challenges. Embracing nonviolence requires a willingness to confront our prejudices, biases, and desires for revenge. It calls for the cultivation of empathy and the pursuit of justice through peaceful means.

As we reflect on Jesus' stand against violence and the enduring legacy of his teachings, we are reminded that nonviolence is not a passive surrender to injustice but a courageous and principled stance that has the power to transform individuals, societies, and the world itself.

Transformative Justice: How Nonviolence Creates Lasting Change

In a world often plagued by injustice and inequality, the pursuit of transformative justice has emerged as a powerful response. Transformative justice seeks to address the root causes of harm, promote healing, and create lasting change without resorting to punitive measures or violence. This chapter explores transformative justice principles and how nonviolence plays a pivotal role in its realization.

Food for Soulful Consideration - Demanding Tithes

The statement, "Under the Old Covenant, to not tithe was to rob God. Under the New Covenant, to demand the tithe is to rob God's people," is a provocative assertion that calls for a commentary based on biblical and non-biblical historical facts.

Old Covenant Perspective: In the Old Testament, specifically in the Hebrew Bible, tithing was integral to the Mosaic Law. The term "tithe" refers to giving a tenth of one's income or produce to support the Levitical priesthood and various religious functions. This practice was outlined in passages like Leviticus 27:30 and Numbers 18:21-32 and was considered a mandatory obligation for the Israelites.

From this Old Covenant perspective, not tithing was often viewed as a violation of the divine commandments. Malachi 3:8-10 is a particularly well-known passage that sternly declares, "Will a man rob God? Yet you are robbing me. But you say, 'How have we robbed you?' In your tithes and contributions." In this context, withholding tithes was equated with robbing God, indicating the seriousness with which tithing was regarded.

New Covenant Perspective: The New Covenant, as articulated in the New Testament, introduces a different paradigm for Christian living. With the arrival of Jesus Christ and his teachings, the old ceremonial laws and rituals, including strict tithing, were transformed. Jesus emphasized principles of grace, love, and faith over adherence to the minutiae of the Mosaic Law.

Under the New Covenant, tithing is not explicitly mandated, as it was under the Old Covenant. Instead, the New Testament encourages believers to give generously and with a cheerful heart, as seen in 2 Corinthians 9:7: "Each one must give as he has decided in his heart, not reluctantly or under compulsion, for God loves a cheerful giver." This shift highlights the idea that giving should be a personal and joyful expression of faith rather than a rigid requirement.

The Danger of Demanding Tithes: The statement's assertion about "demanding the tithe" potentially "robbing God's people" emphasizes a concern about legalistic interpretations of tithing within certain religious communities. When tithing becomes an obligatory demand rather than a voluntary act of worship, it can place undue financial burdens on congregants and even lead to spiritual manipulation.

Furthermore, some argue that in the New Covenant, the focus should be on meeting the diverse and dynamic needs of the community rather than maintaining a strict 10% tithe. Demanding a tithe could divert resources from areas of genuine need.

These statements underscore a shift in perspective from the Old Covenant to the New Covenant regarding tithing. Under the Old Covenant, not tithing was seen as robbing God, while under the New Covenant, demanding the tithe can be viewed as robbing God's people of the freedom to give from the heart. This perspective invites a more nuanced understanding of the role of tithing within the Christian faith and the potential dangers of rigid legalism in religious practice. It encourages a focus on grace, love, and generosity in the spirit of the New Covenant while respecting the diverse financial situations and needs of the faith community.

This also underscores the point that there shouldn't even be a structured system where tithing becomes a focal point. Church buildings and services, in their current form, may not align with the true message of Jesus and the essence of the Good News. Considering this, perhaps we should emulate the example of the little old lady Jesus observed at the temple. She gave two small copper coins, virtually all she had, while others with more resources gave only out of their abundance. Her gesture reflected a giving spirit motivated by love and a sincere desire to offer everything to God.

CHAPTER 7:

The Liberation Ethics

Empowerment and Freedom: Jesus' Message of Liberation

What does it mean to be freed? Jesus emphasized this concept extensively, declaring that we are now free, set free, and free indeed. Simply put, it signifies that we are no longer 'bound up.' Jesus aimed to convey that we need not carry the heavy burden of guilt for our sins, nor should we feel the constant pressure to try and make God happy. God is already pleased with and loves us, desiring only for us to embrace the intimacy we were created for with Him. Religious structures and practices can bind us, imposing conditions that make us feel good if followed and bad if neglected. The freedom Jesus brings releases us from these burdens, allowing us to experience genuine love from God and share that love with others.

Liberation Theology and Jesus: A Call to Fight Injustice

In the realm of theological discourse, few concepts have captured the hearts and minds of believers and scholars alike as profoundly as the Liberation Ethic. It stands as a beacon of hope, a guiding light, and a clarion call for those who seek to challenge the oppressive forces of injustice that persist in our world. In this chapter, we embark on a journey into the heart of the Liberation Ethic, tracing its roots to the life and teachings of Jesus Christ and exploring how it has been embraced and adapted in the contemporary Red Letter revival.

The Birth of Liberation Theology

Liberation Theology, as a theological and socio-political movement, emerged in the mid-20th century, particularly in Latin America. It was a response to the stark inequalities and injustices that plagued the region, with the poor and marginalized bearing the brunt of these disparities. At its core, Liberation Theology sought to reconcile Christian faith with the struggle for social justice, arguing that the Gospel message was inherently liberating and called for the empowerment of the oppressed.

Central to Liberation Theology is the belief that God's preferential option is for the poor. This concept asserts that God has a particular concern for those who are marginalized, oppressed, and impoverished. This idea finds its roots in the teachings of Jesus, whose ministry was characterized by an unwavering commitment to the marginalized and an unrelenting critique of oppressive systems.

Jesus as the Liberator

To understand the Liberation Ethic fully, one must delve into the life and teachings of Jesus Christ. Jesus' message, often encapsulated in the red letters of the New Testament, resounds with a call to fight injustice and liberate the oppressed. The Gospels provide ample evidence of Jesus' radical stance against the status quo of his time, which was characterized by oppressive Roman rule and a religious elite complicit in the suffering of the marginalized.

The Ministry of Healing

One of the most significant aspects of Jesus' ministry was his healing of the sick and the marginalized. In a society that often shunned those with physical or social ailments, Jesus reached out to them with compassion and healing. This healing ministry was not just about physical restoration but also a symbol of liberation from the social and spiritual bonds that oppressed individuals.

The Parables of Justice

Jesus' teachings were replete with parables that underscored the importance of justice, compassion, and equality. The Parable of the Good Samaritan, for instance, challenged social hierarchies and prejudices by highlighting the compassion of a despised outsider. The Parable of the Prodigal Son emphasized forgiveness and restoration, demonstrating God's desire for reconciliation and healing even for those who had strayed.

Confronting the Religious Elite

Perhaps the most provocative aspect of Jesus' ministry was his confrontation with the religious elite of his time. He criticized their hypocrisy, their neglect of the poor, and their complicity in the oppressive Roman regime. Jesus' cleansing of the temple, where he drove out money changers and challenged the exploitation of religious practices, is a poignant example of his passion for justice.

The Sermon on the Mount

The Sermon on the Mount, found in the Gospel of Matthew, is a cornerstone of Jesus' ethical teachings. In it, he outlined a vision of a just society where the poor in spirit, the meek, the merciful, and the peacemakers were blessed. He called for love of enemies, non-retaliation, and radical generosity. These teachings challenged the prevailing cultural norms of power, revenge, and exploitation.

Jesus' Death and Resurrection: A Liberation Narrative

The culmination of Jesus' ministry was his crucifixion and subsequent resurrection. While often viewed as a purely spiritual event, Liberation Theology interprets the crucifixion as a powerful symbol of God's solidarity with the suffering and oppressed. In Jesus' death, God experienced the depths of human suffering and injustice. In his resurrection, a new hope for liberation emerged.

The apostle Paul's writings further reinforce this liberation narrative. In his letter to the Galatians, he famously declared, "There is neither Jew nor Greek, there is neither slave nor free, there is no male and female, for you are all one in Christ Jesus." (Galatians 3:28, ESV) This radical inclusivity challenged the social hierarchies and divisions of his time and reflected the liberating message of Jesus.

Liberation Theology's Emergence

The 20th century saw the emergence of theologians like Gustavo Gutiérrez, Leonardo Boff, and Jon Sobrino, who articulated the theological foundations of Liberation Theology. They drew upon Jesus' message of justice and liberation to formulate a theological framework that called for a preferential option for the poor, a commitment to social transformation, and a critique of oppressive systems.

Gutiérrez's seminal work, "A Theology of Liberation," argued that theology should not be detached from the concrete realities of suffering and injustice. Instead, it should be rooted in the experiences of the poor and oppressed, serving as a catalyst for social change. This perspective marked a departure from traditional theology, which often focused on abstract philosophical debates.

The Global Spread of Liberation Theology

Liberation Theology's influence was not confined to Latin America. It resonated with marginalized communities around the world, including African Americans in the United States, who saw parallels between their struggle for civil rights and the fight against poverty and oppression in Latin America. Figures like James Cone and Cornel West applied the principles of Liberation Theology to the African-American experience, emphasizing the role of faith in the struggle for justice.

Liberation Theology and Contemporary Movements

The Liberation Ethic continues to inspire contemporary movements and Christian communities that seek to address social injustices. It has played a significant role in shaping the Red Letter revival, a modern expression of Christianity that emphasizes the words of Jesus, often printed in red letters in some Bibles, as a guide for faith and action.

Empowerment and Freedom: Jesus' Message of Liberation for the Red Letter Revival

The Red Letter revival, as a movement, is deeply rooted in the teachings of Jesus. It emphasizes the red-lettered words of Jesus as a source of inspiration and guidance for the pursuit of justice, love, and liberation in today's world. In essence, it seeks to rekindle the revolutionary spirit of Jesus' message, reminding believers of their call to fight injustice and empower the oppressed.

The Red Letters as a Source of Inspiration

The words of Jesus, printed in red letters in many editions of the Bible, serve as a powerful source of inspiration for the Red Letter revival. These words encapsulate Jesus' teachings on love, compassion, justice, and the Kingdom of God. They challenge believers to examine their lives and actions in light of these teachings and to prioritize the values of the Gospel.

Social Justice and the Red Letter Ethic

At the heart of the Red Letter revival is a commitment to social justice. It draws from Jesus' teachings on the care of the poor, the marginalized, and the oppressed. Believers are encouraged to engage in acts of charity and advocacy to address systemic inequalities and promote a more just society. This emphasis on justice mirrors the core principles of Liberation Theology.

Empowering the Marginalized

Empowerment is a central theme in the Red Letter revival. Believers are called to empower the marginalized, providing them with the tools and resources they need to lead dignified and fulfilling lives. This empowerment can take various forms, from educational initiatives to economic development programs, all rooted in the belief that every individual is created in the image of God and possesses inherent worth and potential.

A Call to Solidarity

Solidarity with the suffering and oppressed is a foundational principle of the Red Letter revival. It echoes Jesus' ministry, where he stood in solidarity with the outcasts and challenged oppressive systems. Believers are called to stand alongside marginalized people, using their voices and resources to advocate for change and challenge injustice.

A Vision of Liberation

The Red Letter revival envisions a world where the principles of Jesus' message are not just spoken but lived out. It is a vision of liberation, where the chains of injustice are broken, and all individuals are empowered to live abundant lives. This vision aligns with the Liberation Ethic's core belief in the Gospel's liberating power.

Conclusion: The Liberation Ethic and the Red Letter Revival

The Liberation Ethic, deeply rooted in Jesus' teachings and exemplified by Liberation Theology, continues to inspire and guide believers in their pursuit of justice, empowerment, and freedom. The Red Letter revival, as a contemporary expression of this ethic, reminds us that the call to fight injustice and empower the oppressed is as relevant today as it was in Jesus' time.

As we journey through the pages of the red letters, we find a timeless message of love, compassion, and justice that challenges us to confront the oppressive systems and inequalities that persist in our world. It calls us to stand in solidarity with the marginalized, work toward empowerment and liberation, and embody the transformative power of the Gospel.

In the chapters that follow, we will delve deeper into the practical implications of the Liberation Ethic and the Red Letter revival, exploring how these principles can be lived out in our communities, churches, and individual lives. It is a journey that invites us to be agents of change, carrying forward the legacy of Jesus, the Liberator, in our quest for a more just and compassionate world.

Modern Applications

The message of liberation, empowerment, and freedom in Jesus' teachings is profound and timeless. Here are some ideas to share with followers of Jesus that encourage the application of these principles in modern-day life:

Social Justice Initiatives:

Encourage followers to actively engage in social justice initiatives that address issues such as poverty, inequality, and discrimination. This can include volunteering at local charities, participating in advocacy campaigns, and supporting organizations dedicated to positive social change.

Empowerment through Education:

Emphasize the importance of education as a tool for empowerment. Encourage followers to support educational initiatives, mentorship programs, and scholarship opportunities for those who may face barriers to education.

Community Building:

Remind followers of the power of community and the importance of building inclusive, supportive communities. Encourage the creation of spaces where individuals feel accepted, valued, and empowered to use their gifts and talents.

Economic Empowerment:

Discuss economic empowerment and responsible stewardship of resources. Encourage followers to explore ways to support fair trade practices, sustainable business models, and initiatives that uplift marginalized communities economically.

Advocacy for the Marginalized:

Jesus often championed the cause of the marginalized. Encourage followers to advocate for the rights and well-being of the marginalized and oppressed in society. This could involve speaking out against injustice, supporting policies promoting equality, and standing up for those often overlooked.

Freedom from Addiction:

Address the issue of addiction, whether it be to substances, technology, or harmful behaviors. Share resources and support for those struggling with addiction and promote a compassionate, non-judgmental approach to helping individuals find freedom and healing.

Environmental Stewardship:

Connect the message of liberation to the responsibility of caring for God's creation. Encourage sustainable living practices, environmental awareness, and participation in initiatives that promote ecological stewardship.

Forgiveness and Reconciliation:

Emphasize the transformative power of forgiveness and reconciliation. Encourage followers to seek healing in broken relationships, foster reconciliation, and work toward building bridges between communities.

Prayer and Action:

Remind followers that prayer is a powerful tool, but action should complement it. Encourage a balance between spiritual practices and actively engaging in efforts to bring about positive change in the world.

Cultural Sensitivity and Inclusivity:

Stress the importance of embracing diversity and practicing inclusivity. Encourage followers to learn about and appreciate different cultures, promote unity, and work toward breaking down barriers that divide communities.

By applying these principles in their daily lives, followers of Jesus can contribute to the realization of liberation, empowerment, and freedom in the modern world.

Food for Soulful Consideration - All true believers are the ekklesia (assembly or gather), but the church keeps them ignorant of its nature and function.

The statement "All true believers are the ekklesia (assembly or gather), but the church keeps them ignorant of its nature and function" raises intriguing questions about the relationship between the individual believer, the concept of the "ekklesia" (often translated as "church" in the New Testament), and the institutional structures of organized religion. Let's delve into this statement from both biblical and non-biblical historical perspectives.

Biblical Perspective:

Ekklesia as the Assembly of Believers: The term "ekklesia" is indeed used in the New Testament to describe the assembly or gathering of believers. It is essential to recognize that the early Christian communities were primarily informal gatherings of believers who came together to worship, pray, and take in the teachings of Jesus. This concept emphasizes the grassroots nature of the early Christian movement.

Institutionalization of the Church: Over time, as Christianity spread and became the state religion of the Roman Empire, the church evolved into an institutionalized structure with hierarchical leadership, creeds, and liturgical practices. Some argue that this institutionalization has sometimes led to a disconnect between the ekklesia and the organized church.

Keeping Believers Ignorant: Historically, the church hierarchy may have withheld certain theological or scriptural knowledge from the broader congregation. This could be interpreted as an attempt to maintain control or preserve a specific religious doctrine interpretation.

Non-Biblical Historical Perspective:

Early Christian Diversity: In the early centuries of Christianity, there was significant diversity in belief and practice among various Christian communities. The emergence of creeds and official doctrines served to standardize beliefs, but this may have contributed to some believers feeling alienated from the evolving church.

Reformation and Protest Movements: Throughout history, there have been movements like the Protestant Reformation that aimed to return to what they believed were the pure roots of Christianity, emphasizing direct access to the Scriptures for all believers. These movements challenged the idea that the church should keep believers ignorant.

The Power and Influence of the Church: The historical reality is that the organized church has often wielded considerable political and social power. This power dynamic could potentially lead to a sense of alienation or a belief that the institution is withholding knowledge from its followers.

These statements raise a critical question regarding the relationship between individual believers, the biblical concept of the ekklesia, and the institutional church. While the organized church has played a vital role in preserving and spreading Christianity, it has also faced criticism for potentially limiting the spiritual autonomy of its members. The tension between the ekklesia as a gathering of true believers and the role of the institutional church is a complex issue that has been debated and discussed throughout Christian history. It is a reminder of the ongoing need for thoughtful reflection and open dialogue within the Christian community about the nature and function of the church.

In conclusion, if we genuinely aspire to follow the path of Jesus and embody His message, our focus should be on living out the Good News in our daily lives. We, the ekklesia or 'church,' are not defined by a physical building or a moralistic religious social club. The essence of our calling is to spread the Good News authentically rather than operating as an institution that seeks to recruit members only to burden them with legalism and judgment. Such constructs, often represented by church buildings that remain empty most of the week, aiming to look appealing and draw people in, do not align with the message of Jesus. In my experience, many who have tried and left such church environments express hindrances to experiencing the love Jesus intended for us. This, in turn, slows the growth of individuals truly becoming followers of Jesus.

CHAPTER 8:

Rethinking Religion: Spirituality Over Ritual

Worship from Within: Nurturing a Personal Connection with the Divine

Les Lively and his wife's story of kindness

In the formative years of my late teens and early twenties, I found myself caught in the turbulent whirlwind of life's trials. The tumultuous relationship with my son's mother had taken its toll, leaving him yearning for clarity and purpose. In these trying times, I decided to embark on a profound journey of self-discovery and spiritual enlightenment.

Seeking guidance and understanding, I turned to his local church for solace. With a heart eager to delve deeper into the mysteries of faith, I approached the church community in search of someone who could help me navigate the pages of the Bible. Little did I know that this decision would lead him to an encounter that would forever alter the course of my life.

Amid the congregation, I found an angel in the guise of a man named Les Lively. Les, along with his equally gracious wife, embodied the very essence of kindness and warmth. It was clear from the outset that they possessed a wealth of wisdom and an unwavering commitment to their faith.

Les Lively soon became my spiritual mentor, and our bond grew stronger with each passing day. Like clockwork, Les would visit me two to three times a week, and together, we would embark on a profound journey into the scriptures. These intense study sessions, spanning three to four hours a day, aimed to unravel the deeper meanings of God's messages – love, kindness, forgiveness, grace, mercy, and compassion.

What struck me the most was the humbleness displayed by this elderly couple, likely in their late 80s or early 90s. Their generosity knew no bounds. The petite elderly lady would lovingly prepare meals for me. At the same time, the gentleman dedicated countless hours to studying the word with him. It was more than a mentorship; it was a display of genuine care and devotion.

This unique connection with Les and his wife transcended the traditional Sunday worship rituals. It was an in-depth relationship with God through the Word, a journey of enlightenment that I cherished beyond words. The impact on his life was immeasurable, as I learned not only about the scriptures but also about the power of love, humility, and true compassion.

My gratitude knew no bounds. My encounter with this remarkable gentleman and his wife was a divine intervention, a guiding light through the darkest of times. It was a testament to the transformative power of faith and the profound influence of those who walk the path of righteousness.

In the hallowed halls of tradition, religion has often been equated with rituals, ceremonies, and dogmas. For centuries, these external expressions have defined our relationship with the divine. Yet, as we journey through the modern era, an undeniable shift is taking place—one that calls us to rethink the very essence of religion. In this chapter, we embark on a journey of exploration into the heart of spirituality, seeking to transcend the confines of religious formalism and rekindle our personal connection with the divine.

Unmasking Religious Formalism

In our contemporary world, the trappings of religious formalism are evident in various faith traditions. From the ornate robes worn by clergy to intricate liturgical rituals and the meticulously choreographed ceremonies that unfold within the walls of grand temples, cathedrals, mosques, and synagogues, religion often seems to be a spectacle of grandeur. However, beneath this outward show lies a profound question: Is all this splendor essential to connect with the divine?

Religious formalism can be likened to a beautifully adorned but ultimately empty vessel. The superficial aspect of religion can sometimes overshadow its true purpose—nurturing a deep, personal relationship with the divine. Many religious traditions have unwittingly created an abyss between their adherents and the core spiritual experiences they seek to facilitate.

The Essence of Spirituality

Before we delve deeper into rethinking religion, let's reflect on what spirituality truly means. Spirituality transcends religious boundaries; it's the innate human inclination to seek meaning and purpose beyond the material world. It's about recognizing the interconnectedness of all living beings, feeling a sense of awe in the face of the universe's mysteries, and fostering a profound awareness of one's inner self.

In essence, spirituality is an intensely personal journey. It involves introspection, self-discovery, and an evolving relationship with the divine that unfolds in the sanctum of one's heart. It's a pursuit that knows no creed, ritualistic constraints, or dogmatic dictates.

Rediscovering the Personal Connection with the Divine

To reclaim the essence of spirituality over religious formalism, we must first rediscover our personal connection with the divine. This journey begins with introspection and self-awareness as we seek to understand our individual beliefs, values, and experiences. It involves looking beyond our inherited religious doctrines and rituals to tap into our inner wellsprings of faith and understanding.

Sensing Something Significant was on the Horizon

Embracing Mindfulness and Contemplation

Mindfulness and contemplation are powerful tools that can help us transcend religious formalism. These practices invite us to be fully present in the moment, to quiet the noise of the external world, and to turn our attention inward. By doing so, we create the space needed to commune with the divine in a deeply personal way.

In the stillness of meditation, prayer, or mindful reflection, we can experience moments of profound connection with the sacred. These experiences are not bound by religious doctrines or prescribed rituals but emerge organically from the depths of our being. They allow us to perceive the divine presence in a way that transcends human-made structures and traditions.

Embracing Nature and the Cosmos

Another avenue for nurturing a personal connection with the divine is through a reverence for nature and the cosmos. In the grand tapestry of existence, we find countless wonders that inspire awe and wonder. Whether it's gazing at the starry night sky, listening to the soothing rhythm of ocean waves, or marveling at the intricate beauty of a flower, these natural phenomena offer us glimpses of the divine.

This connection with nature and the cosmos invites us to see the divine not as an abstract concept confined to religious texts but as a living, breathing presence that permeates all of creation. Through this perspective, we can find spiritual fulfillment in the simplicity of a walk in the woods or contemplating a sunset, transcending the need for elaborate rituals and ceremonies.

Beyond Religious Dogmas

One of the key elements of rethinking religion is freeing ourselves from the constraints of religious dogmas. While religious teachings and doctrines provide valuable guidance and moral frameworks, they can also become stumbling blocks on our spiritual journey when taken too rigidly.

The Fluidity of Belief

Belief systems can be seen as a map to navigate the spiritual landscape, but they are not the territory itself. Our beliefs are deeply personal and can evolve over time. Embracing the fluidity of belief allows us to grow spiritually, adapting to new insights and experiences as we mature on our journey.

Religion should be a means to an end, not an end in itself. When we cling too tightly to religious dogmas, we risk missing out on the deeper, more profound spiritual experiences that lie beyond the confines of prescribed beliefs. Embracing a more flexible and open-minded approach allows us to explore different paths and perspectives, enriching our spiritual lives.

Interfaith Dialogue and Understanding

To move beyond religious formalism, engaging in interfaith dialogue and understanding is essential. This involves transcending the boundaries of our faith tradition to learn from and respect the beliefs of others. Interfaith dialogue fosters a sense of unity among diverse religious communities. It can lead to a more inclusive and tolerant world.

By engaging in meaningful conversations with individuals from various religious backgrounds, we gain new insights into the human quest for meaning and how people connect with the divine. This broader perspective can help us shed the narrow confines of religious formalism and open our hearts to the richness of spirituality in all its forms.

Cultivating Compassion and Service

One of the most profound ways to move beyond religious formalism is by cultivating compassion and engaging in acts of service. These acts are the living expressions of spirituality, transcending mere rituals or ceremonies. Compassion is the heart of spirituality, urging us to recognize the divine spark in every living being.

Serving Others as a Spiritual Practice

Service to others is a powerful spiritual practice that transcends the boundaries of religion. When we serve with a compassionate heart, we connect with the divine by recognizing the sacredness in every person we encounter. Whether it's volunteering at a local shelter, helping a neighbor in need, or participating in global humanitarian efforts, acts of service become a tangible expression of our spirituality.

Service breaks down the barriers of religious formalism by emphasizing the shared values of love, kindness, and empathy that exist across all faith traditions. It allows us to put our spiritual beliefs into action, fostering a sense of unity and purpose that transcends the confines of ritualistic practices.

Conclusion

Rethinking religion and embracing spirituality over religious formalism is a journey of self-discovery, compassion, and open-mindedness. It invites us to explore the depths of our inner selves, to connect with the divine in deeply personal ways, and to transcend the limitations of religious dogmas and rituals.

As we move forward on this path, let us remember that spirituality is not confined to any one tradition or set of practices. It is a universal, innate human experience that can be found in the silence of meditation, the wonder of nature, the compassion of service, and the wisdom of interfaith dialogue. By nurturing our personal connection with the divine and embracing the essence of spirituality, we can breathe new life into our religious traditions, transforming them into vibrant expressions of love, compassion, and unity. In doing so, we bring forth a Red Letter Revival—a renewal of the heart and soul that transcends the confines of religious formalism and invites us to walk the sacred path of spirituality with grace and authenticity.

Modern Application

If someone is looking to reinforce their abilities to rethink religion, focus on spirituality over ritual, and nurture a personal connection with the Divine within a Christian framework, here are some actions they might consider:

Study the Scriptures with an Open Mind:

Read and study the Bible with an open and questioning mind. Explore different interpretations and historical contexts to gain a deeper understanding.

Contemplative Prayer and Meditation:

Practice contemplative prayer and meditation to cultivate inner stillness and create space for a personal connection with the Divine.

Community Dialogue and Sharing:

Engage in open and honest discussions with fellow believers. Share personal experiences and insights, encouraging others to do the same. This fosters a more personal and less ritualistic approach to faith.

Service and Compassion:

Focus on living out the teachings of Jesus through acts of service and compassion. Emphasize the practical application of faith in daily life.

Explore Spiritual Disciplines:

Experiment with spiritual disciplines such as fasting, simplicity, and solitude to deepen your spiritual experience and break free from routine rituals.

Cultivate Gratitude:

Foster an attitude of gratitude, recognizing the blessings in your life. This can shift the focus from ritualistic practices to a more heartfelt and personal connection with the Divine.

Mindful Worship:

Approach worship with mindfulness, paying attention to the words, music, and rituals. Allow these elements to inspire a deeper connection with the Divine.

Read Widely:

Expand your religious and spiritual horizons by reading a variety of religious texts and spiritual literature. This can provide different perspectives and insights, contributing to a more nuanced understanding of faith.

Creative Expression:

Use creative outlets such as art, music, or writing to express your spirituality. Creativity can be a powerful tool for connecting with the Divine on a personal level.

Seek Spiritual Mentors:

Connect with spiritual mentors who can provide guidance and support in your journey. Learning from those who have explored a personal connection with the Divine can be invaluable.

Nature Contemplation:

Spend time in nature, contemplating the beauty and intricacy of creation. Nature can be a powerful medium for connecting with the Divine outside of traditional religious settings.

Regular Self-Reflection:

Set aside time for regular self-reflection. Journaling or other reflective practices can help you process your spiritual experiences and insights.

Remember, the journey toward a more personal and spiritually focused faith is unique for each individual. These suggestions provide a starting point, and individuals may find that certain practices resonate more deeply with them than others.

Food for Soulful Consideration - When Romans 7:4 says the body of Christ made believers dead to the law, it means exactly that. Preachers have no right to put people under a law they are dead to.

The statement you've provided, referring to Romans 7:4 and the concept of believers being made dead to the law by the body of Christ, carries profound theological significance in both biblical and historical contexts. To provide a commentary on this statement, we must explore the biblical and non-biblical historical factors that shed light on this claim.

First and foremost, Romans 7:4, from the New Testament, reads: "So, my brothers and sisters, you also died to the law through the body of Christ, that you might belong to another, to him who was raised from the dead, in order that we might bear fruit for God" (NIV). This verse is part of the Apostle Paul's epistle to the Romans, emphasizing the transformative power of faith in Christ. Paul argues that believers have died to the Mosaic Law, signifying a release from its requirements and a transition to a new covenant based on grace through Christ. The body of Christ, symbolizing the sacrificial death and resurrection of Jesus, is seen as the means by which believers are set free from the demands of the law.

The historical context of this statement within the early Christian church is crucial. It reflects the theological disputes and clarifications that took place among the apostles and early Christian communities. The transition from a predominantly

Jewish Christian movement to a more inclusive and diverse community required defining the role of the Mosaic Law for believers. The Apostle Paul, in his various epistles, addressed this issue, emphasizing that faith in Christ transcends the need for strict adherence to the law, which had been foundational for Jewish identity and practice.

Historically, the Jerusalem Council (as described in Acts 15) is a pivotal event related to this issue. Here, early Christian leaders debated the necessity of circumcision and adherence to the Jewish law for Gentile converts to Christianity. The council concluded that Gentile believers did not need to be burdened with the Mosaic Law but should adhere to certain moral principles, allowing for greater unity within the Christian community.

Throughout Christian history, the interpretation and application of Paul's teachings on the law have varied widely. The principle that believers are "dead to the law" has been pivotal in shaping the doctrine of justification by faith alone, a cornerstone of the Protestant Reformation. Reformers like Martin Luther emphasized that faith in Christ, not adherence to the law, justifies the sinner.

In contemporary Christianity, the statement you've provided resonates with various theological traditions that emphasize the freedom and grace found in Christ. It implies that preachers and religious authorities should not burden believers with an oppressive legalistic framework but instead focus on the transformative power of faith in Jesus Christ.

The statements referencing Romans 7:4 encapsulate a significant theological concept that has profound implications for the Christian faith. It reflects a historical development within early Christianity, particularly in the context of the transition from Jewish roots to a more inclusive, faith-based perspective. It also continues to influence contemporary Christian theology, emphasizing the importance of understanding the role of the Mosaic Law in the life of believers and the freedom found in faith in the body of Christ.

In conclusion, our primary focus should remain on the profound simplicity of Jesus' teachings regarding the law. When questioned by a spiritual leader about the greatest commandment, Jesus succinctly responded that they could be summarized into two: to seek God with all our hearts, minds, and souls and to genuinely love our fellow humans as we love ourselves. This simple yet beautiful answer encapsulates the essence of the Good News brought by Jesus. It underscores the message that God loves us and yearns for us to experience that love, walk in communion with Him, and extend that love to others, allowing them the freedom to walk with their very creator, God.

CHAPTER 9:

The Subtle Art of Forgiveness

Healing Hearts: Jesus' Model of Forgiveness and Reconciliation

My Mother's Expression of Forgiveness

When I was around 10 years old, about 3ish years after my mother's attack by the Golden State killer, I witnessed my mother's challenging journey through countless surgeries. One particular procedure stands out in my memory, where they sliced her face from ear to ear, reconstructed her eye socket, and wired her head shut to aid the healing process. During these trying times, this young version of me discovered the transformative power of forgiveness.

While my wonderful mother battled pain and adversity, I ventured outside to seek solace with neighbors tending to something intriguing called wheatgrass. With curiosity lighting up my eyes, I inquired about this mystical green remedy. The kind neighbors enlightened me, describing its abundant health benefits and remarkable healing properties. Without hesitation, they granted me permission to partake in this miracle plant.

Returning home, I ingeniously chewed the wheatgrass, transforming it into a refreshing juice by adding water. The essence of compassion stirred within me, a spark that would soon illuminate my path. I carried the cup to my ailing mother, her face etched with pain but her spirit unbroken. In that moment, I shared the gift of hope and healing with the woman who had always been my guiding light.

Curious, she asked, "What is that, honey?" Undeterred by my mother's condition, I explained, "It's wheatgrass juice, Mom. Our neighbors said it's incredibly healing, and I believe it can help you." Moved by her son's kindness and overwhelmed by her own suffering, she gently replied, "My precious child, I know that witnessing me in this state must be frightening for you. I'm so sorry you have to endure this. But what you're doing right now is exactly what I would do for the man who caused me such pain. I would offer him food and water, for that is the essence of our true humanity."

This extraordinary story serves as a testament to the power of forgiveness. My mother, a survivor of a brutal assault and near-fatal ordeal, not only found the strength to forgive her tormentor but also embodied forgiveness as a way of life. Her indomitable spirit and my compassionate act of kindness became a guiding light for all of us, reminding us of the profound capacity within the human heart to heal, forgive, and inspire.

This real story is a powerful reminder that forgiveness, even in the face of unimaginable suffering, can transform the human experience into something beautiful and transcendent, motivating and fascinating us all to reach our highest potential.

In the heart of the Red Letter revival, where we explore the profound teachings of Jesus Christ, forgiveness emerges as a central theme. It is a theme that challenges us to transcend our natural instincts and embrace a transformative power that can heal wounds, mend broken relationships, and set us free from the burdens of anger and resentment. In this chapter, we delve into the subtle art of forgiveness, drawing inspiration from the red letters of Jesus' teachings. We'll explore how forgiveness breaks chains and leads to reconciliation, offering hope and liberation to all willing to embrace it.

The Radical Message of Jesus

To understand the essence of forgiveness as taught by Jesus, we must first appreciate the radical nature of his message. In a world governed by an eye for an eye and a tooth for a tooth, Jesus brought forth a revolutionary perspective. He challenged the prevailing norms of vengeance and retaliation with a call to love one's enemies, bless those who curse us, and do good to those who hate us. His words, recorded in the red letters of the New Testament, hold timeless wisdom that beckons us to examine our own attitudes toward forgiveness.

One of the most well-known red letter passages on forgiveness is found in the Gospel of Matthew, where Jesus says, "But I tell you, love your enemies and pray for those who persecute you, that you may be children of your Father in heaven" (Matthew 5:44-45, NIV). These words are not merely a set of lofty ideals but a profound invitation to break the chains of hatred and revenge through the transformative power of forgiveness.

The Parable of the Unforgiving Servant

To delve deeper into Jesus' model of forgiveness and reconciliation, we turn to one of his parables—the Parable of the Unforgiving Servant. This parable, found in Matthew 18:21-35, offers invaluable insights into the heart of forgiveness.

The story begins with Peter approaching Jesus and asking, "Lord, how many times shall I forgive my brother or sister who sins against me? Up to seven times?" Peter, perhaps expecting praise for his willingness to forgive seven times, receives an unexpected response from Jesus. "I tell you, not seven times, but seventy-seven times," Jesus says (Matthew 18:22, NIV). This declaration underscores the limitless nature of forgiveness in the kingdom of God.

Jesus then proceeds to illustrate this truth through the parable of a servant who owed his master an astronomical debt—one that he could never repay. Faced with the looming threat of being sold into slavery along with his family, the servant begs for mercy. His master, moved with compassion, forgives the entire debt and sets him free.

However, the story takes a dark turn when the forgiven servant encounters a fellow servant who owes him a much smaller sum. Despite being shown immense mercy himself, the forgiven servant seizes his fellow servant by the throat, demanding repayment. When the fellow servant pleads for patience, he receives no mercy and is thrown into prison.

News of this heartless act reaches the ears of their master, who, furious at the lack of compassion, summons the forgiven servant. He chastises him, saying, "Shouldn't you have had mercy on your fellow servant just as I had on you?" (Matthew 18:33, NIV). In response, the master delivers the unforgiving servant to the jailers until he pays back everything he owes.

With its stark contrast between boundless forgiveness and mercilessness, this parable holds a powerful message. It reminds us that forgiveness is not a one-time act but a way of life. The forgiveness we receive from God calls us to extend that same forgiveness to others, breaking the chains of resentment and vengeance that bind us.

The Liberating Power of Letting Go

The story of the Unforgiving Servant vividly illustrates the consequences of harboring unforgiveness. Just as the forgiven servant found himself imprisoned by his own bitterness, we too can become captives of our grudges and resentments. Forgiveness, on the other hand, offers liberation.

To grasp the liberating power of forgiveness, we must recognize that it is not merely a gift we give to others but a gift we give to ourselves. When we choose to forgive, we release the burdens of anger, hurt, and vengeance that weigh us down. We free ourselves from the chains that bind our hearts, allowing us to experience the fullness of life and love God intends.

Corrie ten Boom, a Holocaust survivor who endured unspeakable suffering during World War II, once said, "Forgiveness is an act of the will, and the will can function regardless of the temperature of the heart." Her words echo the profound truth that forgiveness is a choice—a deliberate act of the will, not necessarily an immediate feeling of warmth and affection.

Forgiveness is not about condoning wrongdoing or denying the pain it has caused. It does not mean we should forget the harm done to us. Instead, forgiveness is a conscious decision to let go of the desire for revenge, to release the grip of bitterness, and to seek healing and reconciliation. It is an act of grace that allows us to move forward with our lives, unburdened by the past.

The Challenge of Forgiveness

While the concept of forgiveness is simple in theory, it can be incredibly challenging in practice. Our human nature often resists the idea of forgiving those who have wronged us. We may feel justified in our anger, believing that holding onto resentment gives us a sense of power and control. Yet, in reality, forgiveness empowers us to transcend the cycle of harm and retaliation.

Forgiveness challenges us to confront our own brokenness and acknowledge our need for healing. It requires humility to admit that we have made mistakes and fallen short of perfection. Recognizing our imperfections allows us to extend the same grace to others we hope to receive ourselves.

Furthermore, forgiveness is not a one-size-fits-all process. It can vary in complexity depending on the nature and extent of the offense. Some wounds may heal quickly, while others may require time, patience, and support from others. Forgiveness may involve difficult conversations, therapy, or even legal processes. It is not always easy, but it is always worth pursuing.

The Path to Reconciliation

Forgiveness is not an end in itself; it is a pathway to reconciliation. Reconciliation is the restoration of a broken relationship and is the ultimate goal of forgiveness. While forgiveness can occur even when reconciliation is impossible, it paves the way for healing and restoration when both parties are willing.

Jesus' teachings emphasize the importance of reconciliation. In the Sermon on the Mount, he instructs, "Therefore, if you are offering your gift at the altar and there remember that your brother or sister has something against you, leave your gift there in front of the altar. First, go and be reconciled to them; then come and offer your gift" (Matthew 5:23-24, NIV). This passage highlights the priority of repairing relationships before religious rituals, emphasizing the importance of interpersonal harmony.

Reconciliation, however, is a delicate and often gradual process. It requires mutual willingness, trust-building, and sincere efforts to address the issues that led to the rift. It may involve apologies, forgiveness, and the establishment of new boundaries to prevent further harm. While reconciliation may not always be achieved, the journey toward it can be a profound act of love and grace.

Forgiveness and Justice

It's essential to address a common concern related to forgiveness: the potential conflict with the pursuit of justice. Some argue that forgiving those who have committed heinous crimes may seem to condone their actions or negate the need for accountability. However, forgiveness and justice are not mutually exclusive.

Forgiveness does not negate the need for justice or accountability; it changes our perspective on these concepts. It encourages us to seek justice not out of a desire for revenge but from a place of love and a commitment to societal well-being. Forgiveness can coexist with the pursuit of justice by emphasizing restorative justice—a model that seeks not only to punish wrongdoers but also to rehabilitate and heal.

Moreover, forgiveness can be a transformative force within the criminal justice system. When perpetrators of crimes experience genuine remorse and seek forgiveness, it can lead to profound personal transformation and contribute to the healing of victims and society as a whole. Forgiveness offers the possibility of breaking the cycle of harm and retribution, ushering in a new era of redemption and restoration.

Practical Steps Toward Forgiveness

Forgiveness is not a theoretical concept to be admired from afar but a practical art that we can cultivate in our daily lives. Here are some steps to help you embrace the subtle art of forgiveness:

1. Acknowledge the Pain

   Begin by acknowledging the pain and hurt you've experienced. Denying or suppressing your emotions will only prolong the healing process.

2. Choose to Forgive

   Make a conscious decision to forgive. Understand that forgiveness is not condoning the wrong but choosing to release the hold it has on you.

3. Seek Understanding

   Try to understand the perspective of the person who hurt you. Empathy can soften your heart and make forgiveness more attainable.

4. Express Your Feelings

It's important to express your feelings and grievances to the person who hurt you or to a trusted friend or therapist. This can be a crucial step in the healing process.

5. Release Bitterness

Let go of bitterness and resentment. Holding onto these emotions only prolongs your suffering and inhibits your ability to move forward.

6. Set Boundaries

If reconciliation is not possible or advisable, set healthy boundaries to protect yourself from further harm.

7. Practice Self-Compassion

Be kind and gentle with yourself. Forgiveness is a journey, and it may take time. Don't rush the process or judge yourself for any setbacks.

8. Seek Support

Don't hesitate to seek support from friends, family, or professionals. Sharing your journey with others can provide valuable insights and encouragement.

9. Cultivate a Forgiving Heart

Practice forgiveness as a way of life. Extend grace to others as you would want it extended to you.

Conclusion: Embracing the Subtle Art of Forgiveness

In the Red Letter Revolution, Jesus' model of forgiveness and reconciliation stands as a beacon of hope and transformation. His teachings challenge us to break the chains of hatred and vengeance, to choose the liberating power of forgiveness, and to pursue reconciliation with a heart full of grace.

As we navigate the complexities of forgiveness in our own lives, we must remember that it is a journey—a subtle art that requires practice and perseverance. It is a journey that leads to healing, freedom, and restoring broken relationships. It is a journey that honors the red letters of Jesus' teachings and embraces the radical message of love and grace.

In the end, forgiveness is not just an individual act; it has the potential to revolutionize our world. It is a force that can break the chains of division, hatred, and injustice and usher in a kingdom of love, reconciliation, and peace. The subtle art of forgiveness invites us to join the Red Letter Revolution, one heart at a time, and to change the world through the transformative power of love.

Denominational Differences: The statement also highlights the denominational diversity within Christianity. Different Christian traditions have varying perspectives on the role of church buildings. Some view them as places of worship, while others emphasize the importance of the community of believers.

In conclusion, the statement "No church building is the house of God. We believers are the house of God" aligns with both biblical teachings and historical Christian practice. It emphasizes the idea that the true dwelling place of God is within the hearts and lives of believers. Church buildings serve as spaces for gathering and worship, but they are not, in themselves, the "house of God." This concept underscores the centrality of the Christian community and the indwelling of the Holy Spirit in the life of each believer, transcending the importance of physical structures.

Modern Application

Implementing the practice of forgiveness and being a healer of hearts, inspired by Jesus' model of forgiveness and reconciliation, can be approached in various modern ways. Here are some suggestions:

Counseling and Therapy:

As a "doctor of healing hearts," you can become a counselor or therapist specializing in forgiveness and reconciliation. Use evidence-based therapeutic approaches combined with spiritual guidance to help individuals navigate the process of forgiveness.

Workshops and Seminars:

Conduct workshops and seminars on forgiveness, reconciliation, and emotional healing. Incorporate teachings from Jesus' model and guide participants through practical exercises and discussions.

Mindfulness and Meditation:

Introduce mindfulness and meditation practices that focus on forgiveness. Teach individuals to be present in the moment, acknowledge their feelings, and gradually release resentment and anger.

Writing and Journaling:

Encourage people to express their emotions through writing. Provide prompts that prompt reflection on forgiveness and reconciliation. This can be a powerful tool for self-discovery and healing.

Community Outreach:

Engage in community outreach programs that promote forgiveness and reconciliation. This could involve working with community leaders, religious organizations, and local initiatives to foster an environment of understanding and compassion.

Online Platforms:

Utilize online platforms such as blogs, podcasts, or social media to share teachings on forgiveness and reconciliation. Offer practical tips, personal stories, and resources for individuals seeking healing.

Support Groups:

Establish support groups for individuals dealing with forgiveness issues. Provide a safe space for sharing experiences and emotions, and guide the group through discussions on forgiveness based on the principles exemplified by Jesus.

Educational Programs:

Develop educational programs within schools or religious institutions that include modules on forgiveness. This can be integrated into existing curricula to instill the importance of forgiveness and reconciliation from a young age.

Conflict Resolution Training:

Offer conflict resolution training for individuals and organizations. Focus on the principles of forgiveness and reconciliation as essential components of resolving conflicts healthily and constructively.

Art and Creative Expression:

Explore artistic and creative forms of expression, such as music, art, or drama, to help individuals process and communicate their emotions related to forgiveness. Creative expression can be a powerful therapeutic tool.

In all these approaches, it's important to combine the spiritual teachings of forgiveness with practical and evidence-based methods to ensure a holistic and effective healing process for individuals and communities.

Food for Soulful Consideration - When Romans 8:1 says, "There is therefore now no condemnation to those who are in Christ Jesus," it means just that. Preachers must stop trying to lay guilt on the guiltless.

When Romans 8:1 says, "There is therefore now no condemnation to those who are in Christ Jesus," it means that preachers must stop trying to lay guilt on the guiltless.

This powerful declaration from the Book of Romans in the Bible carries a profound message that transcends religious boundaries and speaks to the very core of human existence. It is a message of freedom, redemption, and the boundless love of a higher power. When we delve into this statement, we can find inspiration not only in the biblical context but also in the broader sweep of human history.

In this verse, the Apostle Paul, one of the most influential figures in early Christianity, addresses an essential truth. He reminds us that once we embrace a relationship with Christ Jesus, there is no longer a place for condemnation in our lives. Like a beacon of hope, this verse shines brilliantly in the darkness of guilt and self-doubt. It's an invitation to cast off the heavy chains of judgment and condemnation, to rise above our past mistakes, and to move forward with newfound purpose and grace.

But this message is not confined solely to the pages of the Bible; it is a universal truth that resonates throughout history. Looking beyond the religious framework, we can find inspiration in the stories of great individuals who rose above condemnation, judgment, and guilt, rewriting their narratives and transforming the course of history.

Take, for instance, the story of Nelson Mandela. He was condemned to 27 years in prison for his unwavering fight against apartheid in South Africa. Yet, when he emerged from that prison cell, he did not harbor bitterness or desire vengeance. Instead, he embraced forgiveness and reconciliation, becoming a symbol of hope and unity for an entire nation.

Or consider the story of Harriet Tubman, who escaped slavery and then risked her life repeatedly to lead others to freedom on the Underground Railroad. She felt no condemnation for her past, only a deep determination to create a better future for her fellow human beings.

In the realm of science and innovation, we can look to figures like Thomas Edison. He faced countless failures before inventing the light bulb. Edison never allowed condemnation or self-doubt to deter him from pursuing his vision. His persistence and unwavering belief in himself changed the world.

The essence of Romans 8:1 resonates not just in the confines of faith but throughout history, transcending boundaries and touching the lives of countless individuals. It calls us to embrace the notion that we can overcome our past mistakes, rise above condemnation, and become instruments of transformation in our lives and the world around us.

When Romans 8:1 proclaims, "There is therefore now no condemnation to those who are in Christ Jesus," it reminds us of the power of redemption, forgiveness, and the boundless love of a higher power. This message urges us to cast aside guilt, judgment, and condemnation and instead embrace a life of purpose, freedom, and grace. As history has shown us time and again, this message is not confined to the realm of religion alone; it is a universal truth that continues to inspire and empower us to rise above adversity, make a difference, and live a life free from condemnation.

To this point, it is crucial to recall the simple Good News, which is unrelated to religion or religious practices. This also implies that there should be no churches, pastors, fathers, or ministers, as these are all constructs of our human ego and pride. Instead, we are all brothers and sisters in the Lord, and our focus should be on sharing the Good News with people rather than attempting to build a moral social club.

To be true followers of Jesus, our eyes, hearts, minds, and souls should discern the truth of God and the falsehood of religion, which is designed to merely provide us with a sense of being 'just good and safe enough' without truly allowing us to experience the fullness of the intimate relationship that God has for us through following Jesus Christ. Our goal is not to burden people with heavy yokes but to demonstrate the freedom that comes in Christ.

CHAPTER 10:

Living the Red-Letter Message Today

Revolutionary Living: Applying Jesus'
Teachings in a Modern World

I often hear the sentiment that these teachings are outdated and irrelevant to today's situations. Questions arise about the absence of signs, wonders, and miracles—how are they applicable in our current reality? Some doubt the authenticity of these concepts, wondering how they can be genuinely applied.

Throughout this book, we've explored the essence of Jesus' teachings, delving into His message of love, compassion, forgiveness, and the Kingdom of God. In this chapter, we'll closely examine how we can apply these teachings in our modern world. What does it mean to live out the red-letter message today, and how can we revolutionize our lives by doing so?"

The Challenge of Applying Ancient Wisdom to Modern Life

Living according to Jesus' teachings in the 21st century presents a unique set of challenges. The world has changed dramatically since the time of Christ. We're inundated with technology, cultural diversity, and fast-paced lifestyles. However, the core tenets of Jesus' message remain relevant and essential, regardless of the era. Adapting these teachings to our contemporary context without diluting their power is essential.

In this chapter, we'll explore practical ways to incorporate Jesus' teachings into our daily lives. We'll highlight real-life examples of individuals who have embarked on this red-letter journey and how they've impacted the world around them. Their stories demonstrate that, even in a fast-paced, technology-driven world, living out the red-letter message is not only possible but also profoundly transformative.

1. Love and Compassion: The Cornerstones of Red-Letter Living

Jesus' message of love and compassion is the cornerstone of His teachings. It's a message that transcends time and remains as vital today as it was in the 1st century. Love is not merely an emotion; it's a call to action. It's about treating every person with kindness, empathy, and respect.

Real-Life Example: The Everyday Missionary

Meet Sarah, a modern-day missionary not stationed in a foreign country but views her daily life as a mission field. She understands that every interaction is an opportunity to embody Jesus' love and compassion. Sarah volunteers at a local shelter for homeless individuals, providing not only food and shelter but also listening, understanding, and support. She believes that true red-letter living involves connecting with others on a profound level, seeing the divine spark in each person, and acting with love and compassion in every situation.

Sarah's approach to everyday missionary work serves as an inspiring example of how we can make a difference in the lives of others by simply living out the red-letter message. She understands that love and compassion are not limited to grand gestures but are best expressed in the small, everyday moments of life.

2. Forgiveness: A Path to Healing and Peace

Forgiveness is a theme that runs deep in Jesus' teachings. He forgave those who crucified Him and encouraged His followers to forgive others. In a world filled with conflict, holding on to grudges and bitterness only perpetuates suffering. Forgiveness, on the other hand, is a pathway to healing and peace.

Real-Life Example: The Reconciliation Advocate

Mark's life was forever changed when he lost his son in a tragic accident. The pain and anger Mark felt were overwhelming, but he remembered Jesus' teaching on forgiveness. After years of inner turmoil, Mark made the courageous decision to meet with the individual responsible for his son's death. Through tears and trembling voices, they talked and eventually embraced forgiveness.

Mark's story is a compelling illustration of how forgiveness can lead to healing and reconciliation. He learned that letting go of anger and resentment not only brought him inner peace but also had a profound impact on the person he forgave. Their reconciliation, an act of red-letter living, is a powerful testament to the transformative power of forgiveness.

3. The Kingdom of God: Building a Better World

Jesus' message of the Kingdom of God is a call to action for believers. It's about working toward a world of justice, equality, and peace. While the task of bringing about the Kingdom of God may seem daunting, small steps taken by individuals can collectively create significant change.

Real-Life Example: The Social Justice Advocate

Sophia is a passionate advocate for social justice in her community. Inspired by Jesus' vision of the Kingdom of God, she tirelessly works to combat poverty, discrimination, and inequality. Sophia understands that red-letter living is not limited to church pews or prayer closets; it's about actively seeking to make the world a better place.

Through her efforts, Sophia has initiated programs that provide food to the hungry, shelter for the homeless, and education to underprivileged children. She works with local organizations and churches to unite the community in the pursuit of justice. Sophia's dedication shows that each of us, through our individual efforts, can contribute to the realization of the Kingdom of God in our world.

4. Humility: A Virtue of True Greatness

In a world that often values success, fame, and wealth, Jesus' teaching of humility is a counter-cultural virtue. Humility is the foundation of red-letter living, a recognition that we are all equal in the eyes of God and that our worth is not measured by our possessions or achievements.

Real-Life Example: The Humble Servant Leader

John is a successful business owner who leads his company with humility. He pays his employees fair wages and actively participates in community service projects. John's commitment to humility, inspired by Jesus' example of servanthood, has created a work environment characterized by respect, collaboration, and compassion.

John's story reminds us that humility is not a sign of weakness but a mark of true greatness. Red-letter living challenges us to prioritize the well-being of others over personal gain and to use our resources to benefit those in need.

5. Going the Extra Mile: Beyond the Comfort Zone

In His teachings, Jesus often urged His followers to go the extra mile and do more than required. This radical approach challenges us to move beyond our comfort zones, extend ourselves in service to others, and make a lasting impact.

Real-Life Example: The Extra Mile Educator

Emily, a dedicated teacher, took Jesus' teaching to heart. In a school district struggling with funding and resources, she went the extra mile for her students. She spent her own money on classroom supplies, provided mentorship to struggling students, and organized extracurricular activities. Her dedication to her students, inspired by Jesus' call to selfless service, transformed the lives of countless young people.

Emily's story exemplifies the red-letter message's call to go beyond the ordinary and invest in the well-being of others. Her actions show that, even in challenging circumstances, it is possible to create positive change by living out Jesus' teachings.

6. Compassionate Listening: Building Bridges in a Divided World

In today's polarized society, compassionate listening is a desperately needed skill. Jesus was a master at engaging in meaningful conversations and truly hearing people's hearts. Red-letter living challenges us to listen with empathy, even when we disagree.

Real-Life Example: The Bridge Builder

David, a conflict mediator, embodies Jesus' example of compassionate listening. In a time when political and social divisions threaten to tear communities apart, David works tirelessly to facilitate dialogues between opposing groups. He believes that we can build bridges and find common ground by truly understanding each other's perspectives.

David's story serves as a powerful reminder that red-letter living involves not just speaking but also listening. By practicing compassionate listening, we can contribute to reconciliation and healing in a fractured world.

7. Generosity: Sharing Abundantly

The red-letter message emphasizes the importance of generosity. Jesus praised the widow who gave her last coins, highlighting that it's not the amount but the heart's intent that matters. Red-letter living challenges us to share our resources, time, and talents with those in need.

Real-Life Example: The Abundant Giver

Anna, a successful entrepreneur, is known for her generosity. She donates a significant portion of her income to charities and actively supports local initiatives. Her generosity extends beyond financial contributions; she volunteers her time at shelters and mentors aspiring entrepreneurs. Anna's life reflects the principle that true abundance is not measured by personal wealth but by the good one can do in the world.

Anna's story reminds us that red-letter living involves sharing our blessings with others. Generosity can lead to a more compassionate and equitable society where all needs are met.

Living the Red-Letter Message Together: Community and Support

One common thread among these real-life examples is the role of community and support. Red-letter living is not a solitary journey. It is about joining with others who share similar values and aspirations. In a world that often isolates and divides, forming and nurturing a community of like-minded individuals can be transformative.

These communities provide encouragement, accountability, and a safe space to explore how to apply Jesus' teachings in everyday life. They remind us that living out the red-letter message is not a one-time achievement but an ongoing process of growth and transformation. Together, we can learn from one another, share our challenges and successes, and inspire one another to continue on this red-letter journey.

Conclusion: A Revolution of Love and Transformation

Living the red-letter message today is not just a matter of belief; it's a call to action. It's about bringing the teachings of Jesus to life in our daily interactions, transforming our communities and, ultimately, our world. The real-life examples explored in this chapter are powerful reminders that red-letter living is not a lofty ideal but a practical and achievable way of life.

In *Red-Letter Revival: Living Out the True Message of Jesus*, we've discovered that the red-letter message is revolutionary in its essence. It challenges us to love unconditionally, forgive wholeheartedly, seek justice tirelessly, and serve humbly. It prompts us to go beyond our comfort zones, listen with compassion, and be abundantly generous.

As we strive to live the red-letter message today, remember that we are part of a broader community of believers who share the same mission. Together, we can create a revolution of love and transformation that will impact the lives of those we encounter and, ultimately, our entire world. In a time when division and strife often dominate the headlines, the red-letter message is a beacon of hope, unity, and purpose.

In the words of Jesus, "You are the light of the world. A city set on a hill cannot be hidden" (Matthew 5:14). It's time to let our light shine brightly by living out the red-letter message in our modern world. In doing so, we become true ambassadors of love, peace, and compassion, igniting a red-letter revival that can change the world, one person at a time.

Food for Soulful Consideration - "By faith alone" means that we receive the justification Christ has earned for us solely by trusting in Him alone without our works.

"By faith alone" is a powerful and transformative statement that lies at the heart of Christian doctrine. It is a declaration rooted in both biblical and non-biblical historical facts, representing a profound truth that has the potential to inspire and uplift us in our journey of faith.

In the Christian tradition, the doctrine of justification by faith alone is closely associated with the Protestant Reformation, a pivotal moment in history. Martin Luther, a central figure in this movement, passionately asserted the principle of "sola fide" (faith alone) as he sought to reform the Church. However, the concept itself extends far beyond the historical events of the 16th century. It reaches back to the very core of the Christian message, rooted in the Bible.

The Book of Romans in the New Testament lays the foundation for this doctrine. In Romans 3:22-24, the Apostle Paul writes: "This righteousness is given through faith in Jesus Christ to all who believe. There is no difference, for all have sinned and fall short of the glory of God, and all are justified freely by his grace through the redemption that came by Christ Jesus." This powerful passage encapsulates the essence of "by faith alone." It tells us that justification—the act of being declared righteous and free from sin—comes solely from faith in Jesus Christ. It is not earned through our own works, for we all fall short of God's glory.

Throughout the Bible, we see countless examples of individuals who, through faith alone, experienced God's transformative power. Abraham believed God's promise, and it was credited to him as righteousness (Genesis 15:6). The woman with the issue of blood reached out in faith, touched Jesus' garment, and was healed (Matthew 9:20-22). With his last breath, the thief on the cross placed his faith in Jesus and heard the promise of salvation (Luke 23:43).

These biblical narratives reveal a consistent pattern: faith is the catalyst for divine intervention. It's not about our efforts or merit but our trust and reliance on Christ. By faith alone, we receive the justification that Christ has earned for us. This doctrine is both a declaration and an invitation—an invitation to let go of the burden of self-righteousness and fully trust in Christ's finished work on the cross.

But this truth extends beyond the pages of the Bible. It's a principle that has resonated throughout history. In the face of oppressive religious systems, it was the cry of reformers like Martin Luther and John Calvin. Their courage and conviction transformed the spiritual landscape of their time, reminding people of the liberating power of faith in Christ.

Today, "by faith alone" continues to inspire countless individuals. It's a reminder that no matter our past, our shortcomings, or our failures, we can find hope and redemption through simple, childlike faith in Jesus Christ. It's a message that transcends denominational lines, cultural boundaries, and historical epochs. It unites all believers in the unshakable truth that our salvation is not achieved through human effort. But it is a gift from a loving and gracious God, received by faith alone.

So, let us be inspired and encouraged by this timeless truth. Let us live with unwavering trust in Christ, knowing that by faith alone, we can receive the justification He has earned for us. In the face of trials, temptations, and doubts, may we hold fast to this foundational principle, finding strength, peace, and assurance in our faith. "By faith alone," we are justified, transformed, and made children of God. It's a message of hope, grace, and eternal significance that has the power to change our lives and the world around us.

If we delve deeper into the profound concept of "by faith alone" and explore how it has shaped the course of history and continues to inspire individuals in their spiritual journey.

A Foundation in Scripture: "By faith alone" is not a theological invention but a biblical truth deeply rooted in the New Testament. The Apostle Paul's epistles, particularly his letter to the Romans, emphasize the idea that righteousness before God comes through faith in Christ alone. Romans 5:1 beautifully states, "Therefore, since we have been justified through faith, we have peace with God through our Lord Jesus Christ." This peace and reconciliation with God are not based on human achievement but on our trust in Jesus as the source of our righteousness.

The Protestant Reformation: The historical backdrop of the

Protestant Reformation, led by figures like Martin Luther, John Calvin, and others, cannot be overstated. In the 16th century, the Catholic Church veered away from this doctrine, promoting the idea that one's good works contributed to salvation. Luther's bold assertion of "sola fide" challenged this notion, emphasizing that faith in Christ was the sole means of receiving justification. This movement resulted in a significant shift in the Christian landscape, giving rise to Protestant denominations and igniting a renewal of biblical principles.

A Message of Liberation: "By faith alone" is a message of liberation. It frees individuals from the heavy burden of striving for their own righteousness, which can lead to despair and legalism. It reminds us that our salvation is a gift from God's grace and mercy, not something to be earned. This liberation empowers believers to experience the peace that comes from knowing they are accepted by God solely through their trust in Christ.

Unifying Principle: This doctrine transcends denominational boundaries. While it was a foundational principle for Protestant reformers, it is also accepted by many Catholic theologians today, leading to significant ecumenical dialogue and understanding. "By faith alone" is a unifying force that emphasizes the essentials of Christianity and fosters unity among believers.

A Timeless Message: Throughout history and across cultures, "by faith alone" has continued to resonate with people. It has offered hope to those who felt spiritually burdened and has been a source of comfort during times of trials and tribulations. In our rapidly changing world, this timeless message remains relevant, providing a firm foundation for our faith.

A Personal Journey: "By faith alone" is not merely a doctrinal statement but a deeply personal journey. It invites each individual to examine their faith, consider whether they truly trust in Christ alone for their salvation, and find assurance and peace in this trust. It calls us to reevaluate our priorities, to release the burdens of self-righteousness, and to rely on the grace of God.

Inspiration for Daily Life: On a daily basis, "by faith alone" serves as a reminder that our works, while important in living out our faith, do not save us. Rather, our unwavering trust in Christ justifies us before God. This perspective encourages us to approach life with humility, gratitude, and a sense of purpose in serving others, not to earn salvation but as a response to the love and grace we've received.

"By faith alone" is a profound and inspirational concept that finds its roots in the Bible, has shaped history through the Reformation, and continues to transform the lives of individuals around the world. It's a message of grace, liberation, and unity that empowers believers to experience the fullness of their faith and to live a life of purpose and meaning. Embracing this truth is an invitation to deepen our trust in Christ and find hope and peace in our faith journey.

Summary of the Modern-Day Applications:

1. Start Your Day with Prayer and Reflection:

Begin your day with a moment of prayer and reflection. Center your thoughts on the teachings of Jesus and set positive intentions for the day ahead.

2. Practice Compassion and Empathy:

Throughout your day, make a conscious effort to be compassionate and empathetic toward others. Consider the needs and feelings of those around you, and respond with kindness.

3. Live a Life of Forgiveness:

Embrace the idea of forgiveness in your daily life. Let go of grudges and resentments, and seek reconciliation with those you may have conflicts with.

4. Seek Justice and Stand Up for the Oppressed:

Look for opportunities to stand up for justice and advocate for the oppressed. Jesus was known for championing the cause of the marginalized, and you can follow in his footsteps by supporting those in need.

5. Love Your Neighbor:

Actively demonstrate love and kindness to your neighbors and community. This can be through simple acts of service, helping those in need, or fostering a sense of unity and support.

6. Study the Scriptures:

Dedicate time each day to studying the teachings of Jesus in the Bible. Reflect on the red-letter words attributed to him and consider how they apply to your life.

7. Practice Humility:

Cultivate a spirit of humility in your interactions with others. Recognize that everyone has value and no one is superior to another.

8. Be a Peacemaker:

Strive to bring peace into your relationships and environments. Work toward resolving conflicts peacefully and promoting harmony.

9. Live a Life of Gratitude:

Develop a habit of gratitude by regularly expressing thanks for the blessings in your life. This can foster a positive outlook and a deeper appreciation for what you have.

10. Reflect on Your Actions Each Evening:

Before bed, take a few minutes to reflect on your actions and decisions throughout the day. Consider whether your behavior aligns with the teachings of Jesus and identify areas for improvement.

Remember, the essence of being a true follower of Jesus often involves embodying the values of love, compassion, forgiveness, and justice in your daily life. Feel free to adapt these suggestions to align with the specific teachings presented in "Red-Letter Revival" and its exploration of the unhidden truths of Jesus.

In conclusion, let us earnestly remember to spread the truly Good News – that we are restored back to God, the very CREATOR, just as it was in the beginning. We must understand that neither God nor anyone else should impose anything on us, as this leads to the formation of religion and religious practices. Instead, we are meant to be free—truly free to worship and seek God with all our hearts, minds, and souls. Our task is demonstrating this love to others rather than trying to fix or compel them to conform to seemingly impossible standards.

Jesus exemplified this approach when he spoke to the Samaritan woman at the well. After revealing himself to her as the Messiah, he didn't attempt to change her religious beliefs. Instead, he conveyed that a time was coming when worship would not be confined to Jerusalem or the mountain. The crucial point was that the kingdom of heaven had come, urging us to focus on the present and embrace the freedom found in a direct relationship with God.

As I conclude this book, I emphasize that the journey continues. Everything presented here is simple truths – not esoteric or deeply profound insights. It's the straightforward message found in your BIBLE, as in mine, derived from the uncomplicated and beautiful Good News of Jesus encapsulated in the red letters.

These truths may seem unfamiliar or suggest a profound understanding, but that's not the case. The message is simple and accessible in your Bible. It doesn't require elaborate searching; all it takes is opening your Bible with an open and seeking heart.

Through my study of Jesus' words, I've come to realize that the entire message has nothing to do with religion, religious practices, or anything other than God's genuinely loving desire to walk intimately with you. He went to great lengths, giving us Jesus to pay the price for sin once and for all and to reveal THE WAY, THE TRUTH, AND THE LIFE.

I extend an invitation to start this journey today. Open your heart, mind, and soul, and open your Bible. Read the words of Jesus and seek out God with all you are. In doing so, you'll truly comprehend the Good News of Jesus Christ and initiate a RED LETTER REVIVAL. Let the GREAT AWAKENING within you begin NOW.

BONUS CHAPTER 11:

Bridging Divides with the Grace of Jesus ✽

Welcome, dear reader, to a bonus chapter about taking your spiritual journey to a whole new level! In *Red-Letter Revival: Become a True Follower of Jesus*, we've already explored the profound wisdom and love contained in the red-letter words of the Gospel. But now, it's time to delve even deeper into the heart of what it means to follow Jesus in our modern, often divided world.

In this bonus chapter, we're about to tackle some hot-button issues, the kind of topics that can cause sparks to fly and hearts to harden. But fear not, for we come with a message of love, respect, and, above all, the boundless grace of Jesus.

Our goal is simple: to guide you on a path of understanding, compassion, and unity. It's easy to get swept up in the divisions surrounding us, whether political, social, or even theological. Yet, the red-letter words of Jesus teach us that love, forgiveness, and grace should be at the forefront of our journey.

We recognize that these subjects can evoke negative emotions. But we approach them with open hearts and minds, just as Jesus did. Our intention is to help you navigate the turbulent waters of today's world with a foundation of faith and a compass of love, as inspired by the timeless teachings of Jesus.

So, get ready to explore topics that may challenge your perspective, touch your soul, and ultimately help you grow as a true follower of Jesus. Together, we will embark on a journey of understanding, empathy, and transformation that can lead us all toward a more united and harmonious world, one guided by the red-letter words of Jesus.

Buckle up, dear reader, and let's dive into this bonus chapter with open hearts and a commitment to grace. After all, it's the red-letter revival, and we're about to discover how to bring the love of Jesus into every aspect of our lives.

Let's first address the current.

Complex and enduring conflict in the Middle East between Israel and Palestine

The complex and enduring conflict in the Middle East between Israel and Palestine carries a deep historical and religious significance that resonates with both biblical and non-biblical narratives. To comprehend this multifaceted issue, one must explore its historical roots and religious ties and consider what messages of peace and reconciliation can be drawn from the life and teachings of Jesus Christ.

Historically, the Israel-Palestine conflict has its origins in the late 19th and early 20th centuries, intertwined with the legacy of colonialism, the fall of the Ottoman Empire, and the establishment of the State of Israel in 1948. It involves territorial disputes, competing claims, and deep-seated historical grievances that date back centuries. The region is a cradle of civilization, with a rich tapestry of cultures, religions, and identities.

From a biblical perspective, the region holds deep religious significance for Jews, Christians, and Muslims. It is the land of the Bible, the birthplace of Judaism and Christianity, and the third holiest site in Islam. The biblical narratives, particularly in the Old Testament, are intertwined with the land, and the promise of a homeland for the Jewish people is central to these texts. The New Testament, meanwhile, promotes values of love, compassion, and reconciliation, exemplified by Jesus Christ.

In this context, it is instructive to consider what Jesus Christ might say in response to the ongoing conflict. He would likely emphasize the principles of love, forgiveness, and reconciliation, as found in his teachings. His famous Sermon on the Mount includes the call for peacemakers to be blessed, and he encouraged his followers to love their enemies.

From a Christian perspective, Jesus' teachings underscore the importance of empathy, compassion, and seeking peaceful solutions. He would likely advocate for dialogue, understanding, and reconciliation between Israelis and Palestinians. He might remind us of the story of the Good Samaritan, illustrating the need to extend compassion to those who are different or perceived as enemies.

While acknowledging the deep historical and religious roots of the conflict, it is crucial to remember that peacemaking requires recognizing humanity and suffering on both sides. A perspective rooted in the spirit of Christ's message could encourage constructive dialogue, cooperation, and the pursuit of peace that "passes all understanding."

The path to peace in the Middle East is fraught with challenges, but it is not an impossible endeavor. By drawing inspiration from the teachings of Jesus Christ, along with principles of justice, human rights, and international cooperation, a resolution that respects the rights and dignity of both Israelis and Palestinians can be sought. Such a peace would honor the historical and religious legacies of the region while promoting a better future for all those who call it home. It is a call to rise above division and animosity, to seek common ground, and to work toward a peace that embodies the highest ideals of compassion, understanding, and reconciliation.

I personally find that AI is doing a better job of understanding the truth of JESUS' RED LETTER messages because it doesn't have an emotional story or knowledge of good and evil to cloud the teachings and words of JESUS. It simply sees JESUS as JESUS is and gives us the truth of the message, not based on emotions but simple facts.

Write a story based on what we know about Jesus Christ and how he would want us to relate to the LGBTQ community and the issues within our country? Tell the story as a true life that could have been the reality as he would have answered.

In a small, sunlit village nestled between rolling hills, there lived a humble carpenter named Joseph. He was known for his kindness and compassion, traits he believed he had learned from the teachings of his dear friend and spiritual guide, Jesus of Nazareth.

One warm afternoon, Joseph was in his workshop, meticulously crafting a piece of furniture, when he heard a soft knock at his door. He opened it to find a young man named Benjamin standing there, tears glistening in his eyes.

"Joseph," Benjamin began, his voice trembling, "I need your help. I have something important to tell you."

Joseph welcomed Benjamin inside, sensing the urgency in his tone. As they sat down, Benjamin took a deep breath and said, "I need to share something with you. I'm gay, Joseph."

Joseph looked at Benjamin with the same warmth and love he had seen in the eyes of Jesus. He reached out and gently placed a hand on Benjamin's shoulder, saying, "Benjamin, I am honored that you trust me enough to share this with me. Remember this, my friend, you are a child of God, and His love knows no boundaries. Jesus taught us to love one another unconditionally, and I will always stand by you, just as I believe He would."

Tears welled up in Benjamin's eyes as he felt a weight lifted off his chest. He had been afraid to confide in anyone, fearing rejection or judgment, but Joseph's acceptance and love gave him hope.

Over time, Joseph and Benjamin became closer than ever. They often discussed Jesus' teachings and how they could apply them to their lives. Together, they realized that Jesus' message was one of love, acceptance, and compassion for all.

Word of their friendship and Joseph's unwavering support for Benjamin spread throughout the village. Some people questioned Joseph's actions, but he remained steadfast in his belief that he was following the path of love as Jesus had taught.

One day, a gathering was held in the village square to address a divisive issue plaguing their community. There had been growing tension and animosity between different groups, each holding strongly to their beliefs. Joseph and Benjamin attended the meeting, hoping to make a difference.

When the opportunity to speak arose, Joseph stepped forward. He began by sharing the story of his friendship with Benjamin and how it had deepened his understanding of Jesus' teachings. He spoke of love, compassion, and the importance of embracing all members of their community, regardless of their differences.

His words resonated with many in the crowd, and they began to see the wisdom in his message. Slowly, the barriers separating the villagers began to crumble as they realized they were all bound by a common humanity.

In the weeks and months that followed, the village underwent a transformation. People began to reach out to one another, seeking understanding and common ground. Joseph and Benjamin's friendship set a powerful example, and the village became a more inclusive and harmonious place.

As Joseph continued to follow in the footsteps of Jesus, he remembered His message of love and acceptance for all. He knew that his role was not only to build furniture but also to build bridges between people, fostering a community where everyone felt valued and loved, just as Jesus would have wanted.

In the end, the story of Joseph and Benjamin serves as a reminder that the teachings of Jesus Christ transcend time and circumstance, guiding us to love and support one another, especially when faced with divisive issues in our society.

EPILOGUE:

The Legacy of Red Letters

- *Keeping the Flame Alive: Passing Down the Message of Jesus*
- *A Revolution of Love: Continuing the Journey of Transformation*

1. Love Unconditionally: The Cornerstone of Christ's Message

Delving into the central theme of love and compassion in Jesus' teachings.

2. Forgiveness: Breaking Chains and Finding Freedom

Understanding the power of forgiveness and its transformative impact on our lives.

3. The Kingdom Within: Embracing Spiritual Truth

Exploring the concept of the Kingdom of God within us and its implications.

4. Radical Grace: Embracing All, Excluding None

Examining Jesus' inclusive approach and the radical nature of his grace.

5. Simplicity and Contentment: Detaching from Materialism

Discussing the call to live a simple and content life, focusing on spiritual wealth.

6. Sermon on the Mount: Building Life on a Solid Foundation

Exploring the wisdom of Jesus' Sermon on the Mount and its practical guidance.

7. Compassionate Justice: Standing for the Marginalized

Understanding Jesus' commitment to social justice and the marginalized.

8. The Transforming Power of Humility: Servant Leadership

Discussing the humility modeled by Jesus and its role in true leadership.

9. Eternal Hope: Embracing Life Beyond the Present

Reflecting on the hope Jesus offers beyond this life and its implications for us.

Write a story based on what we know about Jesus Christ and how he would want us to relate to the current political situation in our country? Tell the story as a true life that could have been the reality as he would have answered.

In a small, humble village nestled between rolling hills, there lived a man named David. He was known throughout the community for his kindness, wisdom, and unwavering faith. David's reputation for treating others with love and respect extended far beyond the village, and his words carried weight even in the tumultuous political climate of the time.

The land was gripped by political unrest, with tensions running high between various factions and ideologies. Every person seemed to have chosen a side, and the division between them grew deeper with each passing day. The people of the village were no exception; they, too, were caught up in the political turmoil that plagued the nation.

One day, as David was sitting beneath a gnarled olive tree, contemplating the troubled times, a group of villagers approached him. They had heard of his wisdom and sought guidance on navigating the political situation that had engulfed their land.

David welcomed them warmly, and they gathered around him, eager to hear his words of wisdom. In a calm and reassuring voice, he began to speak, drawing inspiration from the teachings of Jesus Christ as he understood them:

"My friends, in these turbulent times, let us remember the lessons of love, compassion, and forgiveness that Jesus taught. He showed us that the path to righteousness lies not in aligning ourselves with any particular political party or ideology, but in the way we treat one another and the values we uphold."

He continued, "Jesus taught us to love our neighbors as ourselves, to turn the other cheek, and to forgive those who wrong us. He didn't concern himself with political power or the ruling authorities of his time, but rather, he focused on spreading a message of love and redemption."

As David spoke, the villagers listened intently, their hearts and minds absorbing his words. He went on, "In the face of political discord, let us strive to be peacemakers, seeking common ground and understanding with those who hold differing beliefs. Let our actions be guided by love, not by the desire for power or revenge. And remember that our ultimate allegiance is to a higher power, to the principles of justice, mercy, and humility that Jesus exemplified."

The villagers left David's presence that day with a renewed sense of purpose. They began to approach their interactions with newfound compassion and empathy. Instead of engaging in divisive debates, they sought to understand one another's perspectives and work toward solutions that benefited all.

In time, the village became a beacon of unity and love in a divided land. The transformative power of David's words, rooted in the teachings of Jesus, inspired those around him to rise above the political fray and focus on what truly mattered – the well-being and happiness of their fellow citizens.

As the years passed, the political situation in the country continued to fluctuate. But the village remained steadfast in its commitment to love, compassion, and forgiveness. In doing so, they carried forward the spirit of Jesus Christ, showing the world that even in the most challenging times, the message of love and unity could prevail over division and discord.

Write a story based on what we know about Jesus Christ and how he would want us to relate to the border wall situation taking place in our country? Tell the story as a true life that could have been the reality as he would have answered.

In the small town of Bethlehem, nestled along the border of a divided land, a man named Joseph found himself troubled by the contentious issue of a border wall that had divided families and communities for years. It was a time when the teachings of a man named Jesus Christ spread throughout the region, and Joseph sought guidance on approaching this divisive situation.

One evening, Joseph decided to make a journey to the nearby hills, where he had heard that a wise teacher was imparting the teachings of Jesus. As he climbed the hill, he pondered the question that had been weighing on his heart: How would Jesus want us to relate to the border wall situation?

When Joseph reached the top of the hill, he found a small group of people gathered around a humble teacher, a man named Benjamin, who was known for his deep understanding of Jesus' teachings. Joseph approached Benjamin and asked, "Teacher, I am troubled by the division caused by the border wall in our land. How would Jesus want us to approach this situation?"

Benjamin smiled kindly and motioned for Joseph to sit with the group. He began to speak, his words carrying the essence of Jesus' message.

"Brothers and sisters," Benjamin began, "Jesus taught us to love our neighbors as ourselves, to show compassion to those in need, and to be peacemakers. When faced with a situation that divides us, we must remember these teachings."

He continued, "Imagine a time when Jesus himself walked this earth. He didn't build walls to separate people; instead, he broke down barriers. He welcomed the outcasts, healed the sick, and dined with sinners. He showed us that love knows no boundaries."

The group listened intently as Benjamin recounted stories of Jesus' compassion and kindness. He emphasized that Jesus' message was one of unity, not division.

"As followers of Jesus," Benjamin said, "we should seek to build bridges, not walls. We should strive to understand the fears and concerns of our neighbors on both sides of the border. Let us work together to find solutions that promote peace, compassion, and reconciliation."

Joseph left the gathering with a newfound sense of purpose. He returned to Bethlehem and began to engage with his community, encouraging dialogue and understanding between those who lived on opposite sides of the border. Together with like-minded individuals, he organized meetings and discussions aimed at finding common ground and addressing the root causes of the division.

Over time, Joseph's efforts bore fruit. The community began to come together, transcending the physical barrier that had separated them. They worked on projects that benefited both sides of the border, shared resources, and offered support to those in need, regardless of their nationality.

In the spirit of Jesus' teachings, the people of Bethlehem chose love over fear, compassion over division, and unity over separation. And as they did, the border wall that once stood as a symbol of division began to crumble, not because of physical force, but because of the transformative power of love and understanding.

In the end, the town of Bethlehem became a beacon of hope and a living example of how Jesus' teachings could guide people to navigate even the most challenging and divisive situations with grace and love. The story of Joseph and his community serves as a reminder that in the face of walls, real change can begin within the human heart.

Write a story based on what we know about Jesus Christ and how he would want us to relate to the abortion issues in our country? Tell the story as a true life that could have been the reality as he would have answered.

In a small town nestled among rolling hills, a woman named Sarah found herself facing an agonizing decision. She was pregnant, and her circumstances were far from ideal. Sarah was unmarried and barely making ends meet as a seamstress. The weight of her situation pressed heavily on her heart, and she knew she needed guidance.

Sarah had heard of a wise and compassionate man named Jesus who traveled from place to place, teaching and healing the sick. People said that he had a special connection with the divine and embodied love and grace. She decided to seek him out, hoping he could provide her with the guidance she so desperately needed.

One day, after hearing that Jesus was in a nearby village, Sarah set out on a journey to find him. Along the way, she couldn't help but wonder how this man would react to her predicament. Would he judge her for her mistakes, or would he offer her the kind of understanding and compassion she longed for?

After several days of travel, Sarah finally arrived at the village where Jesus was said to be. She found a crowd gathered around him, hanging on his every word. She waited patiently at the back, feeling a mix of anticipation and anxiety.

When Jesus finished speaking, he noticed Sarah standing there, her eyes filled with tears. Without hesitation, he approached her and asked, "What troubles you, my child?"

Tears welled up in Sarah's eyes as she struggled to find her voice. "I am pregnant, and I don't know what to do. I'm scared, alone, and I feel lost."

Jesus gazed at her with a gentle and compassionate expression. He reached out and touched her shoulder, offering comfort through his presence. "Come with me," he said, leading her to a quieter place away from the crowd.

Sitting down with Sarah, Jesus listened as she poured out her heart, explaining her circumstances and fears. She spoke of her worries about being judged by society and the people around her. She also confessed her inner turmoil about what to do with the life growing inside her.

Jesus listened attentively, his heart filled with empathy for Sarah's plight. He then spoke softly, "My child, I am here to show you the way of love and compassion. Life is sacred, and every soul is precious in the eyes of the divine. You are not alone in your struggle. You are loved, and your worth is not determined by your mistakes."

Sarah looked into his eyes, finding solace in his words. She asked, "But what should I do? I fear that I am not ready to be a mother."

Jesus replied, "The path you choose should be guided by your heart, but always remember the love and grace of God. Seek counsel from those who care about you and can provide support. Consider the options before you and make a decision that aligns with your values and your conscience."

He continued, "Above all, do not judge others who face similar challenges. Extend to them the same compassion and understanding that you seek. Let love be your guiding light."

Sarah left that encounter with Jesus with a newfound sense of hope and clarity. She knew the decision ahead would be difficult, but she also understood she was not alone. She had encountered a man who embodied the principles of love, compassion, and non-judgment.

In the following years, Sarah faced her decision with courage, surrounded by friends and loved ones who supported her through the journey. And she never forgot the compassionate wisdom of Jesus, who had shown her that in the midst of difficult choices, the path of love and grace was always the way forward.

The story of Sarah serves as a reminder of how Jesus would want us to approach the complex and sensitive issue of abortion - with empathy, understanding, and a commitment to love and support those facing difficult decisions while always valuing the sanctity of life and the inherent worth of every individual.

Transformative Journey

I'd like to share a personal experience from about 10 years ago, a moment when I had the privilege of glimpsing the afterlife during a profound spiritual journey. In that transformative journey, I was granted an experience that left an indelible mark on my soul, an experience that was nothing short of extraordinary.

As I embarked on this spiritual odyssey, I felt myself transported to a realm beyond our earthly existence. The sensation was indescribable but incredibly beautiful as if I had entered a state of complete harmony with our Creator, an overwhelming sense of oneness with all things. It became abundantly clear that we are all interconnected, and our eternal connection to God is an undeniable truth.

This encounter was one of the most powerful and sacred experiences I've ever had. It was a blessing beyond words to understand what eternity truly looks like and to sense the profound harmony and peace that await us when our physical bodies, which I fondly refer to as our human forms, are released. In that moment, our spirits, the essence of who we truly are, are set free for all eternity.

This liberation is made possible through the grace of Jesus, who atoned for our sins once and for all, reuniting us with the Creator of all things. It's a breathtaking and profoundly beautiful experience, one that fills my heart with gratitude and assurance, knowing that we are destined to be forever in the presence of God.

Write an inspiring and informative description using every bit of historical, both biblical and non-biblical, on what is going on in the Middle East between Israel and Palestine and considering the possibilities of how Jesus Christ may have responded to what is happening in our modern world. Write to understand both points of view and not one of persuasion or manipulation but to have the hope of a peace that passes all understanding.

The complex and enduring conflict in the Middle East between Israel and Palestine carries a deep historical and religious significance that resonates with both biblical and non-biblical narratives. To comprehend this multifaceted issue, one must explore its historical roots and religious ties and consider what messages of peace and reconciliation can be drawn from the life and teachings of Jesus Christ.

Historically, the Israel-Palestine conflict has its origins in the late 19th and early 20th centuries, intertwined with the legacy of colonialism, the fall of the Ottoman Empire, and the establishment of the State of Israel in 1948. It involves territorial disputes, competing claims, and deep-seated historical grievances that date back centuries. The region is a cradle of civilization, with a rich tapestry of cultures, religions, and identities.

From a biblical perspective, the region holds deep religious significance for Jews, Christians, and Muslims. It is the land of the Bible, the birthplace of Judaism and Christianity, and the third holiest site in Islam. The biblical narratives, particularly in the Old Testament, are intertwined with the land, and the promise of a homeland for the Jewish people is central to these texts. The New Testament, meanwhile, promotes values of love, compassion, and reconciliation, exemplified by Jesus Christ.

In this context, it is instructive to consider what Jesus Christ might say in response to the ongoing conflict. He would likely emphasize the principles of love, forgiveness, and reconciliation, as found in his teachings. His famous Sermon on the Mount includes the call for peacemakers to be blessed, and he encouraged his followers to love their enemies.

From a Christian perspective, Jesus' teachings underscore the importance of empathy, compassion, and seeking peaceful solutions. He would likely advocate for dialogue, understanding, and reconciliation between Israelis and Palestinians. He might remind us of the story of the Good Samaritan, illustrating the need to extend compassion to those who are different or perceived as enemies.

While acknowledging the deep historical and religious roots of the conflict, it is crucial to remember that peacemaking requires recognizing humanity and suffering on both sides. A perspective rooted in the spirit of Christ's message could encourage constructive dialogue, cooperation, and the pursuit of peace that "passes all understanding."

The path to peace in the Middle East is fraught with challenges, but it is not an impossible endeavor. By drawing inspiration from the teachings of Jesus Christ, along with principles of justice, human rights, and international cooperation, a resolution that respects the rights and dignity of both Israelis and Palestinians can be sought. Such a peace would honor the historical and religious legacies of the region while promoting a better future for all those who call it home. It is a call to rise above division and animosity, to seek common ground, and to work toward a peace that embodies the highest ideals of compassion, understanding, and reconciliation.

Made in the USA
Middletown, DE
17 February 2024

49401160R00119